Designs That Stand Up, Speak Out, and Can't Be Ignored:

Promotions

ROCKPORT

GLOUCESTER MASSACHUSETTS

ROCKPORT PUBLISHERS

Designs That Stand Up, Speak Out, and Can't Be Ignored:

Promotions

Lisa Hickey

First published in the United States of America by
Rockport Publishers, Inc.
33 Commercial Street
Gloucester, Massachusetts 01930-5089
Telephone: (978) 282-9590
Fax: (978) 283-2742
www.rockpub.com

Library of Congress Cataloging-in-Publication Data
Hickey, Lisa.
    Designs that stand up, speak out, and can't be ignored : promotions / Lisa Hickey.
        p.   cm.
    ISBN 1-59253-104-0 (hardcover)
    1. Commercial art—United States—History—21st century. I. Title.
NC998.5.A1H53 2004
741.6'023—dc22   2004009993
                                                                                          CIP

ISBN 1-59253-104-0

10 9 8 7 6 5 4 3 2 1

Design: Sussner Design Company

Cover Image: Sussner Design Company

Printed in China

Contents

Introduction

Is it junk or is it not?

There are countless products and services being marketed these days. Every one of those is promoted in some way. The effect can be dizzying. With thousands of companies trying to call attention to themselves, the average person needs to be able to sift quickly through them all to find only the ones that are meaningful. Otherwise, most of us would never make it through the day.

Self-preservation dictates that you need to be able to throw away the junk and remember only what is most interesting. So how does our mind decide what we save and what we don't, what we remember or not? And how do marketers, designers, copywriters, and advertisers make sure that their promotions are the ones that get noticed?

In a discipline that's part art, part science, there are a few rules of thumb. One of the most effective ingredients for a successful promotion is to get the audience involved in some way. Grab them with humor, tactile effects, surprises, interactive measures, and lush and inviting materials or images.

But the best way to tell you how a successful promotion is created is to show you examples. The 75 promotions in this book will cause you to react in some way. They demonstrate how to use concept, copy, design, typography, and materials to their maximum effectiveness. They show you how to promote to different audiences in different ways. They show you a slice of the very best promotional activity that's happening around the world. And they show you what makes a promotion impossible to ignore.

Innovative

All new! Sometimes a promotion is striking for its originality. It gets us to exclaim our appreciation: "Why, I've never seen anything quite like that before!" The sheer newness and freshness of the promotion is what ensures that it will be noticed, appreciated, and remembered.

Design Firm   **Strawberry Frog**
Client   **Onitsuka Tiger**
Project   **Tokyo 64 Hero Breath**

Question: Meditation Session . . .

Close your eyes. Imagine you're at the top of the world. Breathe in, deeply, slowly. Count to three. Now, exhale. Good. You might find yourself using this exercise to relax your mind during a hectic day at the office. Or, if you're a 1964 Olympic gold medalist from Japan, you're probably rehearsing these meditations while breathing into a bag. What for? For canning your breath, of course.

Onitsuka Tiger, an affiliate of ASICS, was releasing a line of athletic footwear called Tokyo 64—shoes commemorating the Japanese gold-medal athletes from the 1964 Olympic Games in Tokyo. So, they asked Strawberry Frog, a design firm in Amsterdam, to spearhead a promotional campaign for their retro soles. The goal was to capture the spirit of the 1964 Games and to create product appeal.

The target audience consisted primarily of European males age 25 to 30 who were opinion-forming individuals. Mark Chalmers, the creative director of the project, provides some psychographic insight into the target audience: "[These people] help define trends and strongly influence early adopters on the street, through their press and social networks." With that in mind, the folks at Strawberry Frog knew they had to come up with a fresh, novel approach that would attract the interest of these young and highly selective trendsetters.

Onitsuka Tiger was releasing a line of athletic footwear called Tokyo 64, shoes commemorating the Japanese gold-medal athletes from the 1964 Olympic Games in Tokyo. The goal was to capture the spirit of the 1964 Games and to create product appeal.

. . . Or Clever Promotion ?

So, late at night with a deadline approaching, the creative team came up with their "Hero Breath" idea, a campaign that would capture the spirit of the 1964 Tokyo Games in the most literal sense. During a limited-time promotion, customers who purchased a pair of Tokyo 64 shoes would take home an aluminum can that would resemble an energy drink container—packaged with the actual breath of 1964 Tokyo athletes.

The process of capturing this "hero breath" involved athletes first reconstructing the 1964 Olympic Games in their minds, then exhaling into a tube that was connected to a bag. This was no hoax—skeptics could visit the official Tokyo 64 website and download a video of these breath-capture ceremonies to see for themselves.

With the canning of the breath such a production, you would think that printing on the cans themselves would be relatively easy. Not so, according to Chalmers, who recalls, "It's easy to print on filled cans. It's less easy to print on a limited run of filled cans. It's almost impossible to print on a limited run of cans containing nothing but breath. We had to be very charming . . ." So, charming they were—charming and clever. And Hero Breath cans they printed.

Answer: A Clever Promotion

The end product was a tangible, handheld advertisement that resonated in people's minds. Both playful and ironic, Hero Breath cans invited consumers to learn more about the Tokyo 64 heritage. And, as a unique and highly collectible item, they quickly made their way into online auctions on eBay.

Now, at the count of three, you will open your eyes, feeling energized and refreshed. If you're a Tokyo 64 athlete just lending a hand—er, a pair of lungs—to the Hero Breath promo, you can stop breathing into that bag now.

During a limited-time promotion, customers who purchased a pair of Tokyo 64 shoes would take home an aluminum can resembling an energy drink container—packaged with the actual breath of 1964 Tokyo athletes.

According to Mark Chalmers, creative director at Strawberry Frog, "It's almost impossible to print on a limited run of cans containing nothing but breath. We had to be very charming."

Close your eyes . . . breathe in, deeply, slowly. Count to three. Now, exhale. Good. You've just re-created a ceremony to can your breath.

Design Firm   **Chimera Design**
Client   **Tennis Victoria**
Project   **Tennis Victoria Annual Report**

How many cups of coffee does it take to come up with a creative breakthrough? Have enough coffee and perhaps it will lead to an idea beautiful in its simplicity—to deliver the annual report for Tennis Victoria, a Canadian nonprofit sporting organization, in empty tennis ball containers.

Follow the Bouncing Ball

The inspiration, besides the coffee, was the client itself. Tennis Victoria wanted to do something that, in its words, was "Strategic Radical," pushing the bounds of creativity while working with very limited resources. The strategy was simple—to position Tennis Victoria as youthful, progressive, and community based. But as if telling the creative team to push the boundaries of creative wasn't enough, the client also delivered a box of tennis accessories, asking if any of the elements could be worked into the final artwork. Imagine the creative team's surprise when they opened the box and discovered an assortment of tennis components including strings, balls, racket fittings, canisters, vibration dampeners, and grips, along with a note that said, "This is everything I could find . . . have fun."

Next came the aforementioned cups of coffee over multiple brainstorming sessions. The tennis ball canisters seemed the easiest way to provide the annual report with a strong visual point of difference and an effective packaging vehicle.

The client delivered their 2002 annual report in empty tennis ball containers—an "ace" concept served up by Chimera Design.

Nothing Is Ever Easy

Of course, as any creative design team knows, nothing is ever really easy. The first challenge was "How many canisters can we get for free?" The answer came several days later when the client rang with an exciting breakthrough: four tennis academies had agreed to donate their empty canisters. In the end, more than 500 canisters were sourced, either metal or transparent plastic, in varying sizes.

Because beggars can't be choosers, the creative team had to deal with the reality of the variations in the containers. The transparent canisters showcased the report and simply required a good cleaning. But the metal tubes were more challenging because they were covered with branding. It was determined that the key to continuity was to produce a single sticker for the metal canisters, which was cut to fit over the existing branding. Matching circular stickers for the lids were also developed.

The printed report itself presented its own hurdles. The cost needed to be kept to a minimum, so the decision was made very early to keep the printing to two color. Having previously developed Tennis Victoria's corporate branding, the creative team knew that the deep blue and yellow green of the logo was a good combination. Experimentation with bold bitmap imaging in the two vibrant colors led to a unique look that felt very "sporting" and the decision was quickly made to use that look throughout the piece.

Recycling Is Good

To further stretch the report's unique look, the decision was made to use a combination of raw brown and crisp white stock. This look also enhanced the underlying recycled theme that came from the use of the recycled canisters. The finishing touch involved binding the report with side singer stitching to imitate a tennis court net and racket strings.

The response from all who received the final piece was invariably, "Wow!" and set the scene for Tennis Victoria to sell itself as the province's premier tennis body.

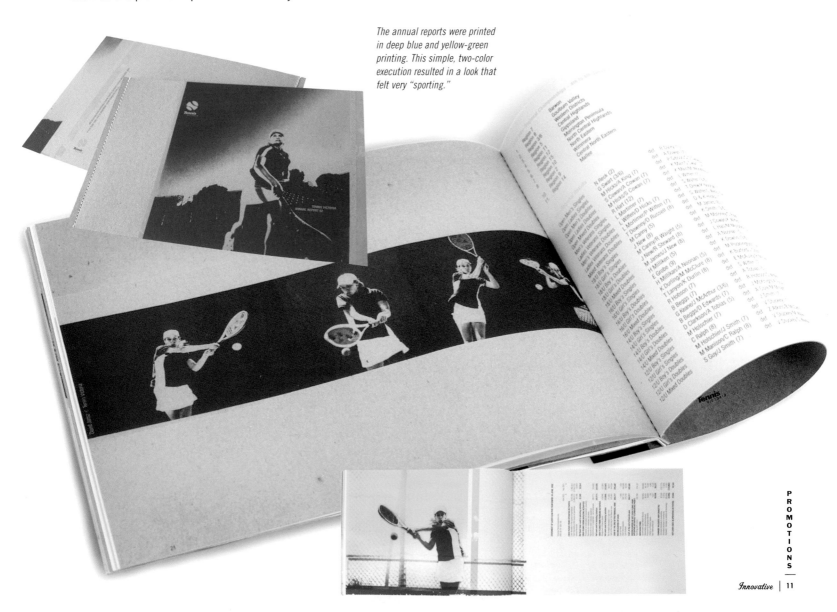

The annual reports were printed in deep blue and yellow-green printing. This simple, two-color execution resulted in a look that felt very "sporting."

Design Firm	deepend
Client	Peroni
Project	Beer Promotion

There's Something about Beer and Girls

A "virtual blond" is used as a promotional device for the Italian beer Peroni. The woman appears, disappears, becomes silhouetted, outlined, and fades in and out. Beautiful and mysterious, she is part of the Peroni brand—a beer that has always used a stylish blond to represent the beer in Italian TV advertising.

The target audience is just about any male old enough to drink—Peroni is enjoyed by people aged 18 to 80. Although the drinkers themselves are predominantly male, research shows that many times it's the female of the house that makes the actual in-store purchase. And there are subtle variations in the target audience, depending on the country. For example, in Italy, Peroni (through its range of beers) appeals to a wide sector of the beer-drinking population—from the supermarket beer buyer to the high-end beer connoisseur. For the rest of the world, Peroni exports limited quantities of beer brands and they are regarded as stylish, fashionable beers. What's mass marketed in Italy becomes a sophisticated import outside of Italy.

The site, then, attempts to have something for everyone, from competitions to win supplies of beer to access to Peroni's legendary TV campaigns dating from the 1960s.

By using a "virtual blond" to promote Italian beer, Peroni stays with a brand that has always used a stylish blond to represent the beer in Italian TV advertising. Beautiful and mysterious, she finds her way onto every page.

More Than Just a Novelty

A novel navigation device allows users to select beers according to lifestyle—V.I.P., Winning, Trendy, and Home & Picnic—and presents a selected range of Peroni's brands relevant to the choice. Another novelty is that the site is built in two languages and Flash dynamically manages the switch—allowing a seamlessly bilingual site that enables users to switch languages on any page. Another interesting feature, in the History and Culture section, is the virtual tour of Peroni's state-of-the-art brewery in Rome—showing how beer is brewed. The brewery schematic was built in 3-D and then exported to Flash for animating. The tour also links through to a series of videos where the user can see actual footage of the real brewery.

The bar games are a simple element to add interesting brand-focused content to the site. The games are styled on the classic bar games of the 1980s—for example, Peronoids pays homage to Asteroids, and Bar Wars recalls Space Invaders. Instead of spaceship graphics, the games feature beer bottles and bar snacks.

Even the look and feel of the site is based on the heritage and strength of the Peroni brand in Italy. There is the strong use of red and gold throughout. The font Clarendon Bold was chosen to present a traditional but friendly face to the site. And, of course, don't forget the ever-present virtual blond!

Users can navigate the site by selecting their preferred lifestyle—V.I.P., Winning, Trendy, or Home & Picnic—and their choice determines which Peroni brands are revealed.

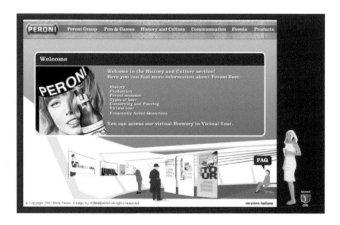

Users can also check out a virtual tour, which takes them through Peroni's state-of-the-art brewery in Rome and shows them the process of brewing beer.

The bar games found on the site are based on classic games of the 1980s. Peronoids is based on the cult favorite Asteroids, whereas Bar Wars recalls Space Invaders. Beer bottles and bar snacks replace the graphics of spaceships from days of yore.

Design Firm **R2 Design**

Client **Teatro Bruto Theatrical Group**

Project ***Krampack* Brochure**

A highly successful play by the name of *Krampack* was making its debut in Spain. The storyline goes like this: Four young friends, three boys and one girl, decide to live together. They install themselves in an apartment and decorate it together. While they are doing this, the quartet continually plays games with each other's feelings. So as the apartment gets progressively better, the relationships between the four of them get progressively worse. By the time all the redecoration is done, they realize they cannot bear to live together under the same roof. At a certain point they actually play Krampack—an invented and very aggressive game they used to play in their childhood.

A promotional brochure was produced by Portuguese design firm R2 for the opening of the critically acclaimed play Krampack.

The brochure features perforated boy and girl paper dolls, which the viewer can punch out and play with.

The Design Team Enters the Stage

Enter, stage left, a Portuguese design firm, R2. Task: to produce an innovative brochure in a very short time and on a very limited budget. This brochure was designed to be given out during the first showing of play the to the press and then sold to the public during the other performances.

The brochure had to be produced in an inordinately short amount of time—one week for concepts and a second week for production. This, however, did not stop the designers at R2 from having a flash of inspiration: the entire brochure for the play would be presented like a game. Because a game is the idea around which the play revolves, R2 wanted to design something that the public could also play at the end. Four paper dolls are perforated into the cover, each one cut into a picture of the actors and actresses. The idea is that people can play with them over the large fold-out apartment drawing that can be found in the middle of the brochure. This drawing is an imaginary apartment based on the actual set.

The program ended up being 16 pages, plus a big vegetal sheet (16¼" x 17" [41.3 cm x 43.5 cm]) and a cover in A5 (5⅞" x 5¼") format. It was offset printed with a Cromo cardboard. The inside was Munken linx paper in two colors, with architecture project paper in one color.

A Standing Ovation

Krampack, the play, premiered at the Sitges International Theatre Festival. It was so successful that Jordi Sanchez was awarded the special prize of the Barcelona critics association. Subsequently, the play toured all over Spain.

The brochure received an equal number of accolades.

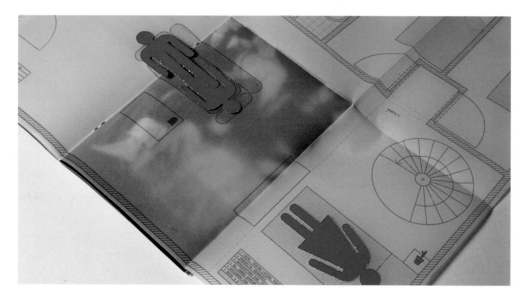

The paper dolls are designed to be used over the illustration of the apartment, which folds out from the middle of the brochure.

The striking visual effect of the doll cutouts is continued throughout the rest of the 16-page brochure.

Design Firm   Amoeba Corp.
Client   Amoeba Corp.
Project   Amoeba Corp. Identity

Amoeba. 1) A single-celled organism. 2) A design firm not afraid of doing things differently and working hard to achieve near-impossible results.

More on the Second Definition

The Amoeba Corp., a design firm in Toronto, Ontario (Canada), was looking to promote itself with an original, innovative, and artistic flair. They wanted to redesign their identity in a way that would highlight the company's multidisciplinary approach to graphic design problem solving. When working for corporate clients, Amoeba must often design around rigid guidelines, yet they are always able to infuse a sense of art into the solutions. Their identity needed to communicate that ability—simply and graphically.

At the cornerstone of the identity are two dot matrix grids that overlap and interact. The rigid grid represents the ordered, systematic methods of problem solving for communications whereas the fragmented grid represents the more artful, creative, though less-structured methods of graphic architecture.

Making It Stand Out

Experimentation ruled the process of design. Unorthodox paper stocks were explored. A variety of different production processes were included to create a more tactile and approachable presentation. Odd color combinations reflect the essence of the company's portfolio, the culture of their youthful client base, and the company's interest in concept over aesthetics.

The business card is the only piece with die-cut holes. Creative director Mike Kelar notes, "We liked the idea of stretching the notion of the matrix on the cards for impact. Even though the grid is formalized in a different manner, the over-all impact is impressive and the relationship to the other forms is apparent and makes sense."

The Amoeba Corp. stationery and signage was a labor of love, experimentation, and trial and error. A variety of printing processes, papers, and production techniques were used.

One piece of the identity considered exceptionally important is the business card. Amoeba believes the business card is the most important piece of stationery. According to creative director Mike Kelar, "It is your spokesperson and billboard when you are not present. It is important that it stand out when placed within the confines of the Rolodex or business card books of potential clients. For this reason, we felt that by indulging in both the design and production of the cards and by taking liberties—which most companies would see as cosmetic and wasteful—we would maximize the potential to stand out and minimize the possibility of not being noticed." The card therefore became the flagship piece of the stationery kit— the smallest piece printed, yet the one with the most dimension and voice.

A Few Challenges

Such an ambitious project is bound to have its share of production problems. Amoeba discovered, for example, that the many production processes caused the paper stocks to become brittle with repeated passes through the printing press. But the biggest hurdle arose from the desire to have a vibrant green printed over the chocolate brown cover stock. Multiple passes of white were required before numerous hits of green could be applied to obtain a color match with the rest of the stationery items. Throughout the process, a number of alternatives were attempted to achieve a bright green on dark brown stock. A green foil would have been an ideal finishing process, but the color did not match to Amoeba's satisfaction. Artistic integrity has a stubbornness all its own.

A Learning Process

Producing something new and different requires a huge amount of patience, cooperation from suppliers, and a willingness to be flexible. As Kelar notes, "We learned a lot along the way, including the way physical properties of paper can have erratic effects on production, and just how much a dark uncoated stock can really absorb ink when trying to match colors." Words spoken by someone who truly believes that hard work can achieve perfect results.

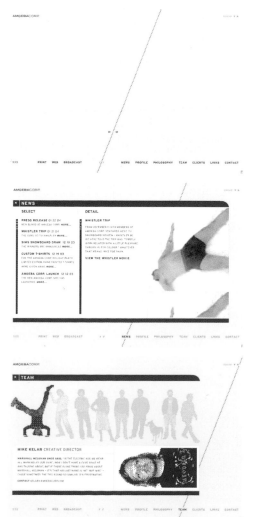

The Amoeba Corp. identity promotion was in production for about a month and in press for two weeks. The overall design required three months of work.

The dot matrix grid was designed to reflect the duality of the company's abilities, and from it all graphic elements are hung. The grid moves, changes colors, and is varied yet retains its integrity across all media.

Design Firm **Terrapin Graphics**

Client **Ontario Federation of Labour**

Project **Safe in Our Lives Brochure**

A Unique Approach

The idea of combining comic book-style illustration with design elements borrowed from Art Nouveau paintings and posters is certainly an interesting design approach. But add to that the subject matter—the prevention of violence against women—and you have a piece unlike anything you've ever seen before.

Terrapin Graphics was called upon by the Ontario Federation of Labour to design a brochure/poster that would alert all women in the province about the escalation of violence against women in the workplace and in the home—certainly a serious issue and not to be taken lightly. Not one where your immediate reaction would be "Oh, I know, comic book art!"

The original strategy to create a brochure and poster originated with Carol-Anne Sceviour, who heads the women's department at the Ontario Federation of Labour and was a client of Terrapin Graphics, an Ontario design shop. One of the key points of the campaign is that the issue of violence against women is not restricted to any sector of society or any special group of individuals. Any woman is a potential victim of violence. Men were encouraged to read the brochure/poster as well. As such, the target audience was everyone in the province of Ontario.

Needless to say, James Peters of Terrapin Graphics took the challenge seriously. But at the same time, he thought it was an opportunity to try something different, to push himself in a design direction he had never pursued before. He notes, "My old style had become so familiar to me that I could produce designs in it without any effort."

And so evolved the comic book-style combined with Art Nouveau. The idea of the patterns was directly inspired by Gustav Klimt's paintings. The patterns add variety to the illustration and help unify the colors through repetition.

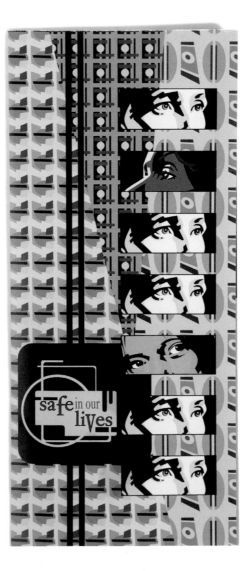

The Ontario Federation of Labour has a department that deals with women's equity issues. This department commissioned Terrapin Graphics to create the Safe in Our Lives brochure/poster to alert all women in the province about the escalation of violence against women in the work-place and in the home.

DESIGNS THAT STAND UP SPEAK OUT AND CANT BE IGNORED

The Client Approves

Because it was the first project Peters produced using this new design and illustration style, he was a bit apprehensive about its reception. He was especially fearful that the client might feel a comic book-style illustration was unacceptable for representing serious issues—that the issue was being treated frivolously. Peters was also worried that the client might simply dislike the design because it was not in the style she was accustomed to from his previous work. Luckily the worries were unfounded. The client noted the change in style but liked it. She particularly liked the cloaks the women in the illustration wore to symbolize the idea of being snug and safe.

Tips from the Heart

Peters has a simple but effective design philosophy. In his words, "There are no bad jobs, only bad design. And bad design occurs when a designer can't find a challenge in even the simplest job. The tendency is to produce a quick and bland design because either the job doesn't pay very much or the designer doesn't like the restrictions imposed by the client.

"I like to think of a client's restrictions as a challenge, a test of my ingenuity. It's the only way to keep a job from turning stale. I love designing and never want it to bore me."

Good advice for anyone who wants to be a design superhero.

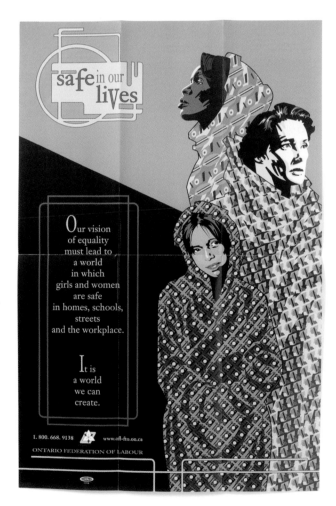

It's easy when you have a good client. Terrapin submitted a single color proof and it was approved by a governmental committee at first pass. No changes were made to the design or illustration. The job went through the printing process without problems and was delivered on time.

James Peters, designer and illustrator, remarks on the style of art chosen: "The kind of comic book art I am fond of is of the old school, in which printing limitations compelled artists to work with flat areas of color. The best of this kind of work is very striking, very dramatic, and has not been improved upon—that's my opinion."

Design Firm   **SullivanPerkins**

Client   **Tuesday Morning**

Project   **Annual Report**

Good Luck, Good Timing

Often great design projects are thought to happen because of good luck and good timing. The annual report for Tuesday Morning is a case in point. While it's quite likely that it would have been a very *good* project no matter what, the fact that it was an annual report for the year 2002 made it *great*.

The whole concept is based on the idea of "looking back, looking forward." An excellent theme. What makes it remarkable is the way it unfolds as the viewer interacts with the piece.

But first, a bit of background.

A Reflection of the Client

Tuesday Morning is a leading closeout retailer of upscale decorative home accessories and gifts, with more than 500 locations throughout the United States. They hold periodic sale events, opening and closing stores during peak buying periods throughout the year, and offering discounted merchandise from top department and specialty stores.

During the past couple of years, Tuesday Morning has wanted an annual report with a clear, concise message for their shareholders. At the same time, they wanted this report to have an innovative, creative approach—not unlike their way of doing business.

_{D E S I G N S   T H A T   S T A N D   U P   S P E A K   O U T   A N D   C A N T   B E   I G N O R E D}

Tuesday Morning is a chain of more than 500 retail stores across the United States. Even on their annual report, designed by SullivanPerkins, they can't help but flaunt the fact that everything is 50 percent to 80 percent off.

Mirror Tricks

So design firm SullivanPerkins was called in. After several meetings with Tuesday Morning, a theme that kept recurring was how the company wanted to reflect on the successes of the past year, yet look forward to new opportunities in the upcoming year. This led to the idea of using an actual mirrored surface as a visual expression of the theme of "Reflections." And in a stroke of good fortune, the year was 2002—a palindrome. A number that can be cut in half on the page and yet appear complete when viewed in a mirror held against the page. The effect is quite, well, remarkable.

The primary target audience is shareholders whose primary interests are the company's performance and its position for future success. Besides containing that information in clear, easy-to-see format, the piece's design reinforced that it was a look back, a reflection, upon the year's performance. A mirror is also, of course, a tool for assessment, for preparing for the future.

The CD included a pdf of the annual report along with the company's 10-K. A printed version of the 10-K accompanied the report when it was mailed.

Initially there was concern about finding a paper that would clearly reflect the "02" and still have a great printing surface. SullivanPerkins was able to find a solution after some diligent research with their local paper company and printer.

The response from shareholders has been quite positive. Rob Wilson, creative director on the project, notes, "When it comes to their annual reports, Tuesday Morning considers it one of the fairest of them all."

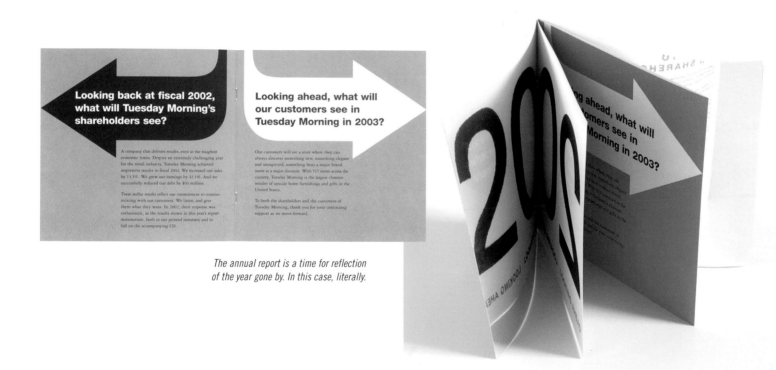

The annual report is a time for reflection of the year gone by. In this case, literally.

The CD attached on the last panel included a pdf version of the annual report along with the company's 10-K.

Design Firm   Dinnick + Howells
Client   Dinnick + Howells
Project   Juxtapose Self-Promotion Cards

Let the Pictures Do the Talking

Holy cow! How do you tell someone they are a sex machine, or tell them to have a great trip, or invite them over for cocktails in a way that's not clichéd?

Don't use words—use pictures. Juxtapose two visual images to create a puzzle that can be funny enough to make people laugh out loud. That was the idea behind the self-promotional cards designed by Dinnick + Howells.

The Juxtapose Cards are a set of cards that the Toronto agency sends to their clients, contacts, colleagues, and friends. Each set contains a dozen or more cards, and they have become a yearly tradition for the design firm. The cards offer a visually rich blend of entertainment, provocation, and usefulness. The idea is for the recipient to be able to pass them along whenever they find that "words themselves are not enough."

The Juxtapose Cards were designed by Dinnick + Howells to "help you express yourself when the right words are difficult to find. We hope you enjoy figuring out and using these images to tell others how you really feel." Cocktails, anyone?

The cards are intended for a visually literate audience that's savvy, urban, and age 25 to 45. Definitely not over the hill.

Assuming a Certain Level of Intelligence

The audience for the cards tends to be those who are familiar with and interested in contemporary design and art, and are, therefore, more visually literate than the regular person on the street. Which is good, because the cards require interactivity to solve, unlike normal, store-bought, pretty cards that come, go, and are quickly forgotten. As creative director Jonathon Howells notes, "Some people get frustrated with them, while others seem to breeze through. It is all the way people are wired." The design firm did realize that the collection from the first year might have been a little too tough to solve. Some were difficult to solve in part because the visuals were either too obscure or of too low quality—the source material is anything and everything, but with a definite preference for "lo-fi" printed ephemera. The cards of year two, although still containing a few doozies, were easier to solve than the first series. Of course, for the indecipherable ones, answers could always be found at dinnickandhowells.com.

Hard Work . . .

The greatest design challenge was finding the exact images needed to support the messages. With access to two of Toronto's best visual reference libraries, designers searched for hours to find the proverbial needle in the haystack. In this case it was more like finding that "perfect old parking lot image that is just bleak and empty enough and is not in color but sepia!" The criteria the designers set for themselves were very tough and unforgiving. The obscurity, yet specificity, of images sought became rather hilarious, especially to bleary-eyed designers who'd had multiple cups of coffee.

. . . Earns Rewards

The response has been very good. The cards have wound up in a number of designer journals and award annuals, and the firm intends to distribute them in design and gallery shops around the world. But the real reward is that people laugh out loud when they finally solve them. Some days, isn't that all you need?

People who are not afraid of being seen as a bit risqué might want to tell someone that they are a sex machine.

"Holy Cow!"

On the back of the cards are these simple instructions: "Just read the pictures and their meanings will appear before your very eyes." The answers are not given on the cards themselves, but people are directed to the Dinnick + Howells website if they get stuck.

Some were designed to offer simple and sweet sentiments to others, such as "Best wishes . . ."

. . . whereas others were intended to be slightly more provocative.

You're a child. You like to play, have fun, and interact with things. You like games that move and include sound. You like characters that are consistent in your life. Although you probably don't have an awareness that you're being marketed to, many people believe that you started to develop a mental image of corporate logos and mascots as early as six months of age. Certainly, by age four you know how to request brand-name products. And once you do, you're as brand-loyal as can be.

Marketing to children is tricky business. There is a special responsibility expected of all marketers to children, but especially those who market to children under age 12. Yet, it's a huge and growing market. By some estimates, if you can create a lifetime customer at an early age, that customer might be worth more than $100,000 to a company over the course of a lifetime.

And nobody knows this better than McDonald's.

Design Firm **Zoesis, Inc.**
Client **McDonald's**
Project **McDonald's Advergame**

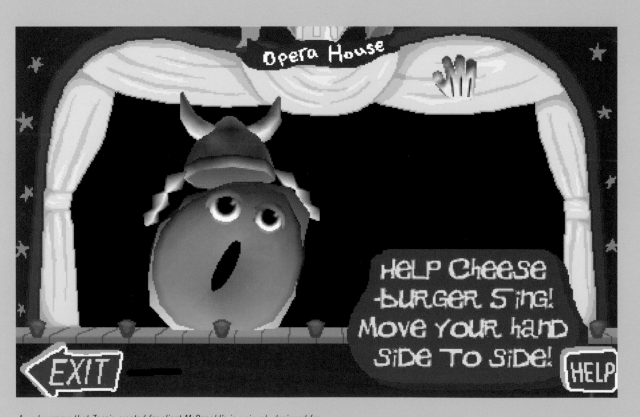

An advergame that Zoesis created for client McDonald's is uniquely designed for the 4 to 12 age bracket. The singing burger will sing faster or slower depending on how fast the child moves the mouse.

When Zoesis, an interactive design firm in Boston, Massachusetts, wanted to design an "advergame" for McDonald's, their strategy was to bring actual products to life in the form of compelling characters. So, for example, a cheeseburger becomes a friendly face with whom children can sing or play tag. By bringing a product to life, kids have the opportunity to make a connection and bond with the product. This bond allows kids to develop positive feelings about the product and the associated brand.

The thinking was simple enough, which is probably why it's such a big hit with the under-12 set. As Laura Elia at Zoesis explains, "We wanted to develop characters that were intrinsic to the McDonald's offering; when you think of McDonald's, you think of burgers and fries."

The other thing they did with this advergame to make it appeal directly to this age group is to make the characters unique and seemingly alive, unlike video games in which characters are wooden and play back scripted animations. The characters react with unscripted emotional and physical responses depending on how kids interact with them. A character will act differently each time a child interacts with it. Because of the awareness of the children's actions, the characters seem more alive.

It is challenging to find ways to get your product into the places where children play. But once you do, just help them have fun!

The actual products, such as cheeseburgers and fries, come to life and interact with the child. The burger and fries take turns being "it" in this game of tag.

Each product is programmed to respond differently depending on how the child reacts. For example, when the child is doing well with the game, the characters will react with big smiles . . .

. . . and when tagged, they will react sadly because the child was able to "catch" them.

Q: It's time for an SAT analogy! Let's see how smart you *really* are (hint: think brand/product associations): Tony the Tiger is to Frosted Flakes as two black speech bubbles are to _____.

A: Well, we didn't actually expect you to figure that one out, so don't feel bad. The word that goes in the blank is NABS, which stands for the National Advertising Benevolent Society. And thanks to Lewis Moberly, a London-based brand engineering firm, the organization now has a new and engaging corporate identity—and one they can be proud of.

NABS' roots trace back to just after World War I as a charity for the advertising industry. Since then, the organization has extended its scope to the entire marketing communications industry. It offers people in the field help and advice regarding employment and personal issues, as well as financial consultation.

Before developing a new corporate image for their client, Lewis Moberly had to determine whom it was, exactly, that the new identity would be appealing to. Nicola Shellswell of Lewis Moberly recalls, "NABS needed an identity to grab the attention of, and be relevant to, a much younger audience who still considered it a 'retirement home for advertising people.'"

ORIGINAL IDENTITY

NEW IDENTITY

Nicola Shellswell of Lewis Moberly explains, "NABS needed an identity to grab the attention of, and be relevant to, a much younger audience who still considered it a 'retirement home for advertising people.'"

DESIGNS THAT STAND UP SPEAK OUT AND CANT BE IGNORED

A Visual Solution

Lewis Moberly's solution was simple, yet immensely effective: dual speech bubbles. But the key was in their graphic orientation—the negative space surrounding the two speech bubbles formed a capital N. Not only was this new logo satisfying to look at, but viewers were rewarded, visually, by noticing how two disconnected elements created a third, and it also revealed what NABS was all about: communication.

Shellswell explains, "NABS now has a language that invites participation. Their website, annual report, presentations, events, and literature are all fully integrated with the identity." The organization's stationery (including letterheads and direct mailers), for instance, embraces the speech bubble graphic as the underlying visual theme; it helps to establish a close relationship between the viewer and the organization.

Because black and white both carry visual impact and are economic to print, Lewis Moberly selected those two colors as the foundation for the design work they did for NABS. However, they later introduced orange as a secondary color to enliven the graphics and, as Shellswell explains, "to add warmth and vibrancy."

The Results Are In

Thanks to NABS' new corporate image, donations increased by 20 percent, 75 percent of which were from new corporate donors. Those donations, in turn, helped the organization reach out to 20 percent more people than in the previous year. Not bad for a simple logo makeover.

Okay, ready for another pop quiz? This time, it should be easy: How does the following headline relate to NABS' new corporate identity?

"New Appearance Boasts Simplicity!"

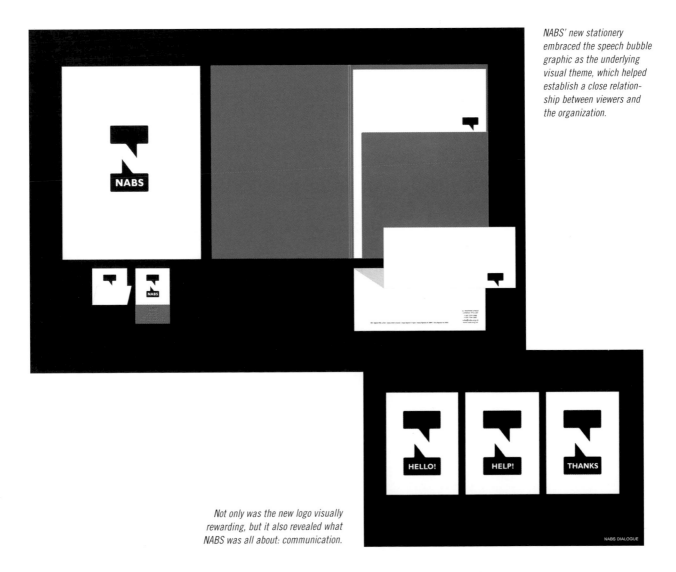

NABS' new stationery embraced the speech bubble graphic as the underlying visual theme, which helped establish a close relationship between viewers and the organization.

Not only was the new logo visually rewarding, but it also revealed what NABS was all about: communication.

No "Air Quotes" Here

Combine a Swiss reinsurance company, a new initiative called The Centre for Global Dialogue, and an internationally recognized English design firm, and what do you get? A stunning identity system in which the cornerstone idea is oversized quotation marks that come together in the shape of the Swiss flag.

Not that it was easy.

"The hardest part of any job is coming up with the right idea, and this was no exception," states designer Matt Willey. "However, once we had developed the graphic using quotation marks in the shape of the Swiss flag, everything else just clicked into place. It was one of those beautifully simple ideas that just worked."

The Centre for Global Dialogue was founded by leading international reinsurance body Swiss Re as a forum for events, programs, and conferences dealing with global risk issues. The facilities and services offered by the Centre attract business leaders, politicians, risk analysts, and other industry experts from around the world.

The design challenge set forth to Frost Design was to develop a corporate identity that would convey the role of the Centre, the diversity of its facilities, and its relationship with Swiss Re clearly and consistently across all promotional material. The solution needed to "appeal to a broad, industry-based audience, while retaining a 'human' element to reflect the nature of the Centre's activities."

DESIGNS THAT STAND UP SPEAK OUT AND CANT BE IGNORED

Since its inception in 1994, Frost Design has grown into a multiaward-winning, internationally recognized graphic design studio, renowned for its bold approach and distinctive use of typography.

Communication and quality are the inspiration behind Frost Design's stunning new corporate identity for the Centre for Global Dialogue in Switzerland.

Dunja Zivkovic
Communications & Branding

Telephone +41 1 704 88 59
Fax +41 43 282 88 59
Dunja_Zivkovic@swissre.com

Swiss Re
Centre for Global Dialogue

A Solid Identity

Niels Viggo Haueter at Swiss Re explains further: "At the Centre for Global Dialogue we deal with a range of complex risk and financial services related issues. So when defining the specifications for our new visual identity we were looking for an expression that helps to structure our topics and activities rather than complicating or confusing the content. At the same time it needed to express an invitation for dialogue at the Centre."

Central to the new identity is a distinctive logotype derived from the Swiss flag, using speech marks as the framework. The speech marks are inspired by dialogue and interaction, key characteristics of the Centre. This graphic forms a grid that can be used on a range of material and literature, from stationery to conference reports to menus and price lists. In fact, it's exactly the type of solution Frost Design is known for—a bold approach with a distinctive use of typography.

Design Approach

The Centre has been designed to the highest standards with strong emphasis on quality and attention to detail. Frost's solution reflects this by using the best quality materials; innovative design for print; and a simple yet bold color palette of red, black, white, and gray. The materials are also recyclable or biodegradable wherever possible, to demonstrate the Centre's commitment to the environment, a subject of major concern in risk assessment.

Vince Frost, who led the project, said, "I have always been inspired by 1950s and 1960s Swiss design, which is based primarily on clean, simple lines and strong grids. With this project I wanted to acknowledge this heritage and create a logo that was worthy of the building and its surroundings."

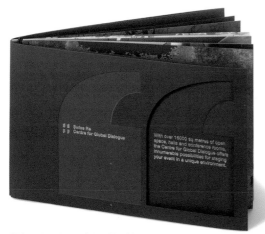

"This project is proof that identities can be design led rather than strategically numbed," notes Vince Frost, creative head at Frost Design.

A variety of papers and materials are used, all recyclable or biodegradable where possible, to keep with the Centre's ideals.

The design grid is based on the simplest of elements—the grid of the Swiss flag.

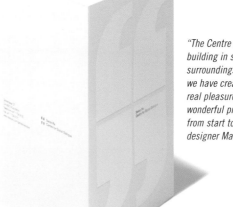

"The Centre is a fantastic building in stunning surroundings and to see what we have created at work is a real pleasure. This was a wonderful project to work on from start to finish," says designer Matt Willey.

Design Firm   Bubblan Design

Client   Stiftelsen FöreningsSparbanken Sjuhärad Bank

Project   Stiftelsen Promotion

A Generous Client

A bank in Sweden wanted to create a continuous promotional campaign that would visualize and provide identity to the bank in an innovative and engaging way. But this is more than the story of innovative design. It is the story of how a bank can give back to the community in ways that are also innovative and engaging.

Stiftelsen is head owner of the bank FöreningsSparbanken Sjuhärad. As a bank owner, he gets a certain amount of money; he gives this money back to local projects that help develop Sjuhäradsbygden, a part of western Sweden. The projects awarded are both small and large, in the areas of science and research, culture, trade and industry, and sports. Over the past six years, Stiftelsen has given in total an astounding 67 million crowns (nearly 9 million US dollars) to projects in the area.

The bank soon realized that this was a competitive advantage and should be marketed as such. No other bank has a Stiftelsen. But the irony was, apart from those who actually received money at the annual celebrations, nobody knew anything about Stiftelsen—not even that he existed.

This intriguing series of images is designed to symbolize the many projects that Stiftelsen, head owner of the Swedish bank FöreningsSparbanken Sjuhärad, helps to support. The pole represents Stiftelsen's support for the projects he assists, which are represented by the growing tree.

Everything Symbolic

So Bubblan Design was called in to promote the fact that the bank had a Stiftelsen as a symbolic force. They did so with a series of intriguing images. At the center of the illustrations was a stanchion, or pole, which symbolizes Stiftelsen. The posters had four parts, which showed a progression of the growth of a plant up the stanchion. Each part symbolized the growth of the projects, the people, and the community that Stiftelsen helped.

Additionally, every spring Stiftelsen has a grand evening when the selected projects are awarded and the money given. Stiftelsen wanted to give a gift to every project, as a memento for years into the future. The gift: a 12 cm by 12 cm (about 5" by 5") black cube, handmade from stoneware with a 6 cm (about 2½") seeding made of soft plastics. An illustration of this was also used as a symbol in printed matter, badges, bags, and T-shirts at the celebration.

Stiftelsen also wanted to give awards of honorary distinction to projects that were extremely well developed. Bubblan's idea was an apple with a stairway, symbolizing the fact that learning is a journey with steps you must take to reach your goal.

The apple is larger than normal and was made of ceramic clay and wood. With so many to create and each one handmade, it was impossible for the artist to make the apples look the same. But the design firm came to a resolution; because the receivers and their projects are all unique, so is the apple—a material that is living and individual.

Everyone engaged in the project with Stiftelsen realizes that it takes time to enter the minds of people. The bank wants to be known as a company that takes part in society, inspiring the possibility to develop positively, for a long time to come. Still, there are some immediate results to report. For example, the day after the latest awards were given, Stiftelsen got their biggest media attention ever.

Generosity becomes a seed for so many things.

Bubblan created a black stone cube with a plastic seedling growing out. This was used both as poster illustrations . . .

. . . and as actual gifts to the recipients of Stiftelsen's generosity.

Another object created to promote Stiftelsen and the bank is this ceramic and wood apple, signifying the steps taken while learning.

"What is rubbish to some is useful to others."

Abandoned wardrobes covered with political statements don't often make a promotional vehicle. But thanks to design firm Carter Wong Tomlin and client Howies, a clothing company, they made quite an exceptional one.

A Joint Effort: Part 1

Howies is a small, ethical clothing company based in Wales. A married couple, David and Clare Hieatt, started the company determined to link their beliefs with their products. Environmental consciousness, organic farming, less dependency on nonrenewable energy sources, and recycling were some of the many things they wanted not only to practice but to spread the word about.

Carter Wong Tomlin used abandoned wardrobes as an innovative point-of-sale promotion for clothing company Howies.

All the wardrobes were deliberately kept quite raw and unfinished, apart from the illustration. Each was fitted with a basic neon light tube, mirror, and label explaining the particular theme.

When commissioned to create point-of-sale, fourteen illustrators responded to the brief, which was to interpret a different "Howies Belief" onto an actual wardrobe.

A Joint Effort: Part 2

An innovative way to do that came in the form of a project to design a point-of-sale piece that could house T-shirts in stores. Howies turned to Carter Wong Tomlin, which had just designed the packaging for those shirts. The packaging's theme revolved around discarded furniture that kids use as ramps and other trick-inducing obstacles for skateboarding and BMXing. Carter Wong Tomlin thought it would be a good idea to carry this theme through to point of sale but wanted to push it further.

Phil Carter, creative director and principal of Carter Wong Tomlin, and a believer himself in the dictum that one more bike is one less car on the road, was making his daily cycling commute to his studio. He started to first notice and then photograph various pieces of abandoned furniture that he passed. Carter liked the idea of these pieces appearing out of context and started to mull *Inside Out* as the potential title for a book.

But suddenly it occurred to him that the abandoned wardrobes would make a perfect promotional vehicle for Howies. The wardrobes were found in a variety of places—highways underpasses, dumps, and in junk shops for £20 or less.

A Joint Effort: Part 3

Carter then involved good illustrator friends (friends being the operative word—being a small company, Howies isn't cash rich) by bribing them with Howie's T-shirts and the promise of good PR. Then, the word spread to other interested parties. The artists were given a list of themes and beliefs dear to Howies, and they chose the one they wanted to do. All in all, fourteen wardrobes were created.

The project took about four months from concept to fruition. Carter Wong Tomlin had the artists come into the studio, which was a bit like having an artist in residence and great fun for all their designers. All the wardrobes were filmed in 360 degrees on slow time video and can be viewed on the Howies website.

Carter Wong Tomlin insists it doesn't have a philosophy; it's a design firm that just wants to do work that pushes the client as well as create work that's innovative. But most importantly, they want to have fun and enjoy designing. Carter says, "I usually take this as a good sign of good work if you've really enjoyed the process of doing the project, the wardrobes being a case in point." But it doesn't hurt to try and make the world a better place while you're at it.

The target audience was Howies customers, who are environmentally aware teenagers mainly into skateboarding, biking, and other adventurous pursuits. The wardrobes were used to house organic T-shirts, whose packaging Carter Wong had also designed.

Creative director Phil Carter ended up getting into the act, designing a wardrobe himself with the assistance of two of his colleagues. His "belief" illustrates the probable extinction of the sparrow if things don't change.

On this wardrobe, Jeff Fisher illustrates Belief #3: "Reclaim the streets. A bike is one less car on the road. The air we breathe is choking us as cars have been proven to cause asthma."

Design Firm	**R2 Design**
Client	**Alexandra Martins**
Project	**Identity**

The Importance of Proper Punctuation

Everyone agrees that punctuation is important. But how many would think to turn it into an entire promotional identity? That is a question worthy of both a question mark and an exclamation point, is it not?!

Alexandra Martins is a journalist responsible for the public relations and public management of important Portuguese businesses. Her company is a relatively small PR firm that works for big companies, and she promotes and organizes events, provides most of the clients' communication needs, and does everything related to successful promotions.

The simple yet effective color scheme of black, cyan, and silver is in keeping with the sophisticated tone. It also reinforces that feeling that much of communication hinges on the writing.

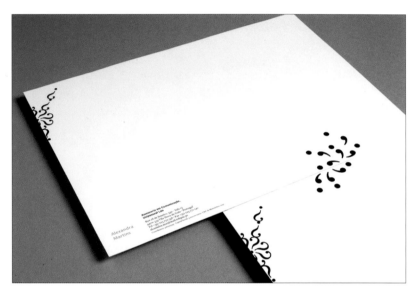

This set of stationery using punctuation marks as graphic elements promotes Portuguese PR maven Alexandra Martins in a surprising way. Because much of what she does is write texts, this was a clever and appropriate concept for her identity.

The Gestalt of It All

So an identity program where commas, periods, question marks, and exclamation points dance across the page and come together in a gestaltlike fashion—an identity where the sum is greater than the parts—seems particularly fitting.

R2, a design firm in Matosinhos, Portugal, started with the idea that although what Alexandra Martin does on the big picture level is communicate and promote business concepts, what she does most often on a day-to-day basis is simply write texts. From there it was a quick conceptual step to thinking of punctuation marks as a bold yet lovely graphic element. According to Liza Ramalho, who directed the art of the project along with designers Artur Rebelo and Nadine Ouellet, the use of punctuation marks "generated truly organic forms that had symbolic meaning alone but even more meaning when viewed together." The punctuation marks "work like a germ," linking several different promotional components together. When placed side by side, for example, the back of a business card fits together with a sheet of stationery-like puzzle pieces. One is reminded of a sophisticated design exercise done in an advanced typography course.

An Elegant Look

The stationery was printed using offset printing on a rich paper stock called Munken Linx. It was printed in three colors: black, cyan, and silver, which was designed to keep with the elegant and sophisticated tone suggested by the design. Plus, the black-over-white paper conceptually reinforces the writing perspective.

Amazingly enough, the entire project took only three weeks from start to completion. It was one of those seemingly magical projects that fell together perfectly. Just two weeks for the creative and design process and one week for the printing. And then it was done, period. Exclamation points, anyone?

The pieces work together in unexpected ways to create a whole that is greater than the sum of its parts.

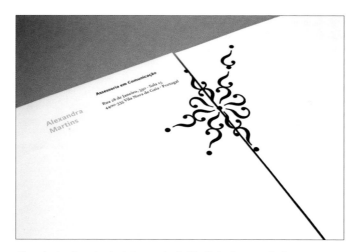

Elegant, stunning, visual—but conceptually it's all about communication.

The entire project took a mere three weeks from brief to printed pieces.

People are visual creatures. So while you can tell them things like "Hey, if we continue to pollute our waterfront, bad things will happen," it's never quite as effective as actually showing them.

Which is precisely why this promotion is so effective.

Devastating Visuals

In just 60 seconds, one gets a vision of devastation far greater than words could explain. Through a clever use of collage animation, a beautiful bay area is transformed into a seething, dirty, industrial mess. The mess is then cleaned up, and a much better solution is put in place before the viewer's very eyes.

An innovative promotion often comes out of an innovative message. Betterbay is an ambitious, ongoing project put on in part by the Army Corps of Engineers, whose goal is to enhance Galveston Bay in Houston, Texas, both environmentally and economically through the responsible and creative use of materials dredged during the expansion of the Houston-Galveston Navigation Channel.

An idyllic landscape appears on screen in this Flash piece created for the ongoing project Betterbay. The Army Corps of Engineers heads this project in an effort to enhance Galveston Bay in Houston, Texas.

Gradually, the scene becomes cluttered with machines, pollution, and industrial waste, until the scene is a virtual wasteland.

Email for More Information

The original strategy of this project was to develop a brief, intriguing teaser that would drum up interest in the viewer about the project and drive him or her to a website for more information. The project was intended to be an embedded Flash piece (400 x 300 pixels) that would be emailed to anyone interested in receiving information about the project as well as anyone of relevance as decided by the client.

The target audience included anyone who would be interested in finding out more about better air and better water, and the effect they have on people. People residing in the surrounding areas of the project, who would be directly affected by the process, were also part of the target audience.

Using Recycled Materials

Metal fabricated the entire scene out of elements from a variety of still photos.. The scrapped and collaged technique gives the whole piece a slightly surreal look. It's a creative, metaphorical representation of progress handled responsibly, which in a nutshell sums up the project. The time-lapse treatment is something that has yet to be tackled in this medium, which makes it unique.

As Peat Jariya, principal and creative director at Metal, notes: "The birth of the idea was actually a result of several brainstorming sessions concerning how to convey the project goals in a captivating, atypical way. We had explored several different directions and decided that this one was the most interesting and effective."

Producing the piece ended up being quite a challenge, and most of the challenges involved file size. Metal knew they had to keep it within a reasonable range or else the viewer would have difficulty downloading the spot. They overcame the problem by limiting the number of layers of activity in the scene as well as editing the piece to only the crucial frames necessary for the spot to work.

The other challenge was figuring out how to do the technique itself. One of the most interesting things about this project is that the treatment resembles a time-lapse movie in which a camera is set up at a designated spot and rolls for an extended period of time to show what was captured in an extremely accelerated way. They were able to capture this feel by using only collage technique and stop-motion animation.

Jariya concludes, "We were pleased with the results. We feel we were able to address the original objectives in a very brief spot. It not only is aesthetically pleasing, but effectively shows the goal of the Betterbay project."

The scene starts to reverse itself.

The scene ends with a reversion back to the original landscape with the addition of very civilized buildings in the background. In this case, the picture truly is worth a thousand words.

Design Firm Strawberry Frog
Client HoeGaarden
Project Promotional Beer Campaign

Want to Try a New Beer? Take a Seat.

Who could imagine that the best way to promote a beer might be by building furniture? The folks at Strawberry Frog, a design firm in Amsterdam, that's who.

The beer is HoeGaarden, and the design firm had gotten the brief to introduce the brand to the opinion-forming audience. HoeGaarden's audience is young and spirited—guys and girls in their twenties and thirties, predominantly working in creative and media industries. This was an audience whose members had a refined genuine taste, who were into art and music, who made it their mission to stay one step ahead, and who have a finger on the pulse of underground culture.

Getting a Share of Headspace

The HoeGaarden brand itself had a lot going for it—it had been around since the 1400s so it had a lot of heritage, and it has an unusual but refreshing taste. It was equally popular among men and women. And it had as one of its brand values the single word "curiosity."

The design firm took an interesting approach. They didn't consider the rest of the beer market as competition. Instead, they looked at other things that provoked curiosity, other things that "took up the headspace" of their audience, as Mark Chalmers, creative director on the project explains. So instead of looking at other beers, they looked at what other items provoke curiosity—art, fashion, books, magazines. And, yes, even furniture.

Looking at it this way, the design firm realized that people would be able to come across the beer through the things that they loved.

Who could imagine that the best way to promote a beer might be by building furniture? The folks at Strawberry Frog, a design firm in Amsterdam, that's who.

Custom-designed furniture was built by Droog Design, an internationally recognized collaboration of Dutch designers. The installation then traveled around Europe, creating little venues in which the beer could be sampled by the target audience.

Welcome to the HoeGaarden

And so an idea was born. Take the brand value of curiosity and combine it with the hottest summer on record for 100 years, and the Strawberry Frog team just couldn't resist the opportunity to make the beer garden and café terrace fashionable again. And thus began the "Welcome to the HoeGaarden" campaign. Custom-designed furniture was built by Droog Design, an internationally recognized collaboration of Dutch designers. The installation then traveled around Europe, creating little venues in which the beer could be sampled by the target audience. As Chalmers notes, "Communicating the need for six foot 'high chairs' for adults wasn't always easy." The end result is festive and captivating, and even includes such touches as a bird feeder that dispenses nuts that can be enjoyed with the beer.

How well did the furniture promote the beer? Incredible buzz and PR were generated. The initial investment was tripled in terms of PR coverage received. And within the first months, the promotion achieved its objective of site visits and signups. But the true value was in the brand loyalty achieved—the audience was surprised and delighted, and appreciated a brand that could talk to them in the right way, playing to their interests in an authentic way, without overselling. According to Mark, this is an agency philosophy: "If we can make you smile, have a bit of fun, we've done a pretty good job—consumers respond best to brands that have fun."

Have a seat, and welcome to the HoeGaarden. And don't forget to smile.

The end result is festive, captivating, and even includes such touches as a bird feeder that dispenses nuts that can be enjoyed with the beer.

Have a seat, and welcome to the HoeGaarden. And don't forget to smile.

Fun. Sophisticated. Lively. Clever. Good-looking.

Sound like your perfect soulmate? Yes? Well, how about your perfect furniture catalog? Wink design knows that just as people have personalities, so do objects. And just like a personality trait can cause us to like or dislike a person, it can cause us to like or dislike mere objects, furniture included. Wink thus tries to create brands that "inspire people to relate to them."

The Brand Personality

Blu Dot is a furniture design and manufacturing company that offers high-end products at accessible prices. Besides being a company that offers "design you can actually afford," they also believe that they have a brand personality that is "clever, sophisticated, and modern." When Blu Dot approached Minneapolis-based Wink to create a catalog for them, they wanted it to not only express their unique brand personality but to have a modular and easily updated grid, and a modern and contemporary tone and feel.

"It all starts with a great product, but the personality of the company and the product needs to come across in every aspect of brand," states Wink founder Richard Boynton.

Blu Dot's bright orange binders are designed to be impossible to miss when looking at the shelves of furniture distributors.

The accordion fold inserts make the whole program modular and easily updated.

Wink's solution was an orange binder with each product line on its own three-hole punched, accordion-folded section. The orange is not only a fun and lively color, but it also "can easily be spotted on nearly all their distributors' shelves." The accordion-folded section allows future additions to be printed and added with ease to the end of each section. Each individual section conveys a specific tone and feel that plays off the sensibility of the various furniture lines themselves. The wit and sophistication of the company's personality comes through in the catalog's humorous copy and unusual propping choices. This entertaining writing, along with the vivid orange binder and the inspirational aspect of the furniture, has made the promotion nearly impossible for distributors to throw out.

Creating Personality Through Humor

This idea of the personality of a company being shown through its catalog is perhaps the most interesting part of this project. The fact that the personality of the Blu Dot designers is contained within the product descriptions of the furniture show that this company's personality, spirit, and creative expression are consistent. According to Wink, most of the time, a client will say that they want it to sound like them but then back off and revert to something a little more safe. However, with Blu Dot, "all of the humorous bits" that Wink threw in, they kept, "which is shocking as some of the lines are pretty ballsy," the designer confesses. For example, how many catalogs would have products with names like "felt up chair" or "flip me table?" Or describe a bookshelf as perfect for "books that you're looking for but cannot see, despite the fact that they're right in front of your face?"

Wink claims that it has been recently pointed out that much of their work tends to be "clever, compelling, and witty. This might be attributed to the fact that we don't try to remove our personalities from the process." These words seem to sum up the success they had with Blu Dot's catalog. Wink knows how much we associate ourselves with brands. Fun? Smart? Sleek? What brands do you associate yourself with?

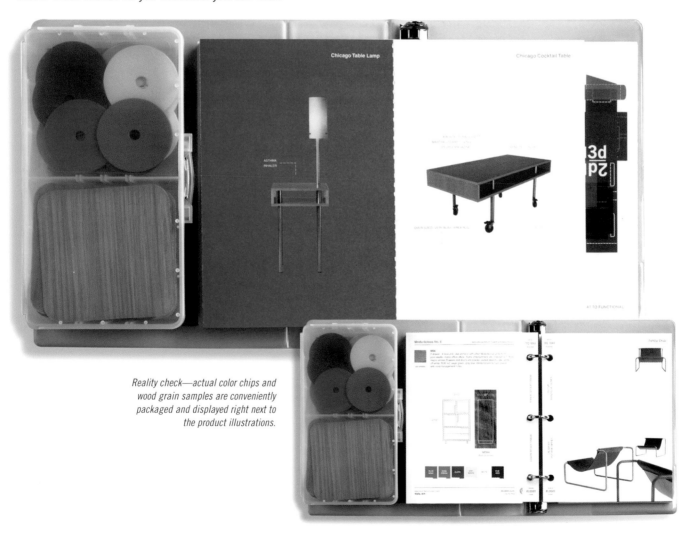

Reality check—actual color chips and wood grain samples are conveniently packaged and displayed right next to the product illustrations.

Humor

Go ahead, laugh. That's exactly what the designers of these promotions would like you to do. And the louder and heartier, the better. It's hard work being funny, but the hard work pays off in these cases. And laughter, as you know, is good for the soul.

Design Firm   **Nesnadny + Schwartz**
Client   **Cleveland Institute of Art**
Project   **Cleveland Institute of Art Direct Mailer**

Turning a Cookie Cutter Industry on Its Head

When you're an institution trying not to look like an institution, what do you do? Look like an institution, of course.

The ultimate challenge for every marketer is breaking through the clutter to reach a particular target. For a college or university not named Harvard, trying to reach students thinking about their next matriculation is particularly difficult. Most institutions seemed to have resigned themselves to slapping together materials with photographs of students perched atop library bell towers and mascot-laden rugby shirts laid out on campus lawns. Leave it to a small art school in the Midwest and their design shop to change the way recruitment campaigns are handled.

For a new system of direct mail material, the Cleveland Institute of Art (CIA) wanted a concept that would "challenge the audience, be courageous, and set a new standard for college recruiting materials." They wanted the piece to create such a buzz that it would almost become a keepsake for the students. To achieve these lofty goals, the designers at Nesnadny + Schwartz determined that they would need to appeal to their audience with a sense of familiarity, while packing an element of surprise. Their solution? A whimsical parody of a standardized test.

Anxious high school seniors can't relate to an average college brochure like they can to a Mad Lib.

An Innovative Way to Break the Ice

The potential problem with this concept was that while every prospective student could identify with it, the likelihood that they would discard it was high as well. At first glance the two-color mailer looks like an SAT booklet, with a pocket holding different weights of papers inside. However, upon further inspection, one quickly sees that it is an interactive platform, with fill-in-the-blank answers to seemingly straightforward questions. In Mad Lib fashion, the inside reveals a quick, first-person narrative about a high school senior's angst about getting into school, with the answers from the straight-forward questions on the front, filling in the blanks. This was the hook to get people in, and in focus groups students loved the fact that, unlike most college brochures, the CIA actually took the time to "break the ice."

Inside the piece, the standardized test parody continued and expanded, with large type, over-the-top word problems, and common symbols to guide the reader to "continue" and eventually "stop" for the answers. All of this reflected the unapologetic message of the CIA, which of course, came in the form of a multiple-choice question:

The Cleveland Institute of Art is:

      a) Five years of hard work

      b) Fun but intense

      c) What you make of it

Of course, it's "d) all of the above." Much like their recruitment brochure.

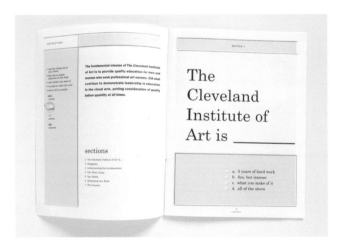

The brochure spelled out the Institute's unapologetic message in no frills, multiple-choice fashion.

Turns out, this is not your parent's SAT booklet. A vibrant, 14-page color insert waits inside the brochure, just in case anyone takes things a little too literally on the outside.

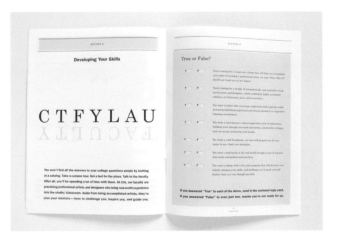

"True or False? You belong at the Cleveland Institute." Some early applicant screening in section 6.

Design Firm **Dotzero Design**

Client **Bridgetown Printing**

Project **Calendar**

"Hey mom, the trip's great. I farmed some fields of real Wisconsin cheese and climbed a big building in Seattle to get some coffee at the top. Too bad everything at home isn't as exciting as it is on the road, and I'll think of you when I ride in a real Oklahoman tornado. Love, your exploring son."

Dotzero Design needed to promote Bridgetown Printing. It seems like an ordinary task. But it could be quite daunting— how do they keep the name Bridgetown Printing in front of customers year-round, attract attention, be seen as high quality yet fun to work with, keep the price of the promotion low, and advertise the fact that the company had sister companies across the country—all in a creative way?

The answer came in the form of monthly calendar installments.

Greetings from Texas! Y'all come back now, y'hear!

The humorous illustrations, reminiscent of retro postcards, were created by using collages of a variety of found and free art.

A Yearful of Quirky Visuals

Dotzero, of Portland, not Bridgetown, Oregon, initially sent each client a metal stand useful for calendar display. Then, each month, the client received that month's calendar, with a "big visual piece on one side and the dates of the month on the other." Because the visuals of the calendar are so fun and unique, they not only catch the eye of clients, but also keep them looking forward to the monthly installments to see what the new month would bring. The calendar expanded on the idea that Bridgetown Printing had sister companies all over the country by using a fictitious traveler traveling the country. Each month had a funny, kitschy photo depicting an American city, using the CEO's photo and containing a humorous message from him to his mom about the city. Dotzero used bright color palettes to further the visual of retro "old hand-tinted photograph vacation postcards."

Funny and Offbeat

Although Dotzero knew that they wanted to incorporate the idea of a calendar arriving in monthly installments, it was a harder task to figure out the pictures the calendar would contain and the feelings they wanted the visuals to evoke. They also knew they wanted to avoid the standard "scenic" pictures, but shooting their own pictures of the cities were out of budget. Brainstorming sessions brought up the idea of having a traveling character "telling about each place in a novel way." They finally finalized the fictional character, the "funny and offbeat" postcards, and the message the CEO would write home every month. However, to assemble the visuals in the way they wanted while staying on budget, Dotzero needed to get really creative. By sampling a little bit of everything and making good usage of the cut and paste method, the monthly visuals were born by assembling copyright-free images such as pieces of old magazines, photo albums, and catalogs. Whoever thought collages were only good for middle-school art projects must have never laid eyes upon a final Dotzero Design calendar. Bon voyage, and keep the postcards coming home.

Each month Dotzero also delivered a corresponding postcard that could be mailed out to continue the grassroots effect of the promotion.

The Bridgetown Calendar is an inventive way to keep the Bridgetown Printing Company in the minds of current and potential clients.

A die-cut card in the shape of the United States explains the concept to recipients.

Design Firm **Cahan & Associates**

Client **Stroock**

Project **Recruitment Campaign**

Lawyers. The butt of a million jokes. (Question: What do you call 50 skydiving lawyers? Answer: Skeet.) And yet the perception is that they take themselves seriously. Way too seriously.

Can Lawyers Be Funny?

When Cahan & Associates was asked to do a promotional recruitment campaign for Stroock, a law firm in San Francisco, they decided to adopt a tone not often heard in the hallowed halls of an elite law firm. Luckily, they had a client who was very receptive to that. Together, the law firm and design firm decided they wanted to break away from the way firms usually talk to candidates. They wanted to avoid language full of promises and clichés about who they will be working with, what they will be working on, how much they will get paid, and how long/hard they will be working. The goal was to create a buzz among top recruits at local law schools. And the campaign succeeded in doing just that.

In fact, the tone they adopted could almost be called, of all things, honest. For example, the cover of the brochure reads, "You are about to become a lawyer. Think about it: This may be the last time anyone is totally up front and 80 percent honest with you."

You are about to become a lawyer. Think about it: This may be the last time anyone is totally up front and 80 percent honest with you.

In a recruitment campaign for the San Francisco law firm Strook, Cahan & Associates created a tone that evokes a word not usually associated with lawyers: honest.

As a first year, you may feel like a fire hydrant. Here, at least you're a well-respected fire hydrant.

STROOCK

Join us at stroock.com

According to Bella Banbury, the account director on the project, research showed that students were frustrated by materials from firms that "all looked the same" and "all said the same thing."

To start, Cahan & Associates researched the mindset of students looking to land a job in their first law firm. According to Bella Banbury, the account director on the project, research showed that students were frustrated by materials from firms that "all looked the same" and "all said the same thing." We also found that materials are not readily available—often the only place to find brochures from different firms was in the library. This helped the design firm decide not only on the voice but on the different components of the promotion and how they were distributed. Cards and booklets were placed in student lockers, and around campus, posters and booklets were used at recruitment fairs, gift packets were given to candidates that interviewed, and the Web component of the campaign was made available to all students online.

The look of the campaign was interesting in several ways. It was not slick in the way you'd expect materials from lawyers to be. One-color, unusually graphic photography was printed on uncoated stock. And in many of the pieces, it wasn't immediately obvious who the law firm was. The goal was to attract the students' attention and get them interested first. It worked!

Who's Laughing Now?

The campaign was a huge success. It resulted in an increase in applications for Stroock and a positive response from schools, recruiting officers, and students. It won a prestigious award from the Legal Marketing Association. It drove students to the website. It created a buzz. And maybe, just maybe, it got one lawyer to take himself or herself a little less seriously. After all, as one line from the promotion states so eloquently: "Now that's something you don't often hear in the halls of a law firm: Laughter."

The Stroock Summer Associate Program: Glamorous work, lavish meals, theatre tickets. Your basic deal with the devil.

STROOCK

Join us at stroock.com

The campaign was a huge success. It increased applications for Stroock, won awards, and created a buzz. And maybe, just maybe, it got one lawyer to take himself or herself a little less seriously.

Design Firm   Renegade Marketing Group

Client   Panasonic

Project   People Against Fun Campaign

Do as You're Told . . .

Don't have fun! Fun is no good and must be avoided at all costs! And whatever you do, don't buy Panasonic products because they will cause you to have way too much fun!

Propaganda? Promotion? Fun?

People Against Fun is a fictitious (thank goodness), sarcastic, witty, online promotion created by Renegade Marketing Group for Panasonic. It was created in response to a strategy stating that the Panasonic brand needed to be "coolified." The strategy needed to get males 18 to 24 years old to love the Panasonic brand. This demographic is the MTV generation that has made extreme sports popular, and has grown up watching edgy shows like *Jackass* and *Punk'd*. This generation has also grown up with computers and Internet access and has a sarcastic, even caustic, sense of humor, and responds best to irreverent and self-deprecating humor.

. . . Or Not

So here's a target audience that questions authority and does not like living with restrictions or being told what to do. They are increasingly independent and marketing savvy, but remain cynical of mass messaging and corporate commercialism. Their disdain for their parents, their teachers, and our leaders fuels their skepticism. People Against Fun, with its spokesperson, Bob Paffersen, are parodies of the killjoys they resent and rebel against. And so the target appreciates and is more likely to identify with a brand that pokes fun at itself.

The People Against Fun was part of a bigger promotion being run by Panasonic called "Save Your Summer," which directly talked about the fun that Panasonic products could deliver. But therein lies the dilemma faced by the creative team. It quickly became apparent that it's very difficult to talk about fun to the teen and young adult audience—the very act of saying you are fun makes you "unfun" in the eyes of such a cynical target. So Renegade Marketing Group brilliantly turned this liability into an asset and "unfun" became the cornerstone of the online efforts.

DESIGNS THAT STAND UP SPEAK OUT AND CANT BE IGNORED

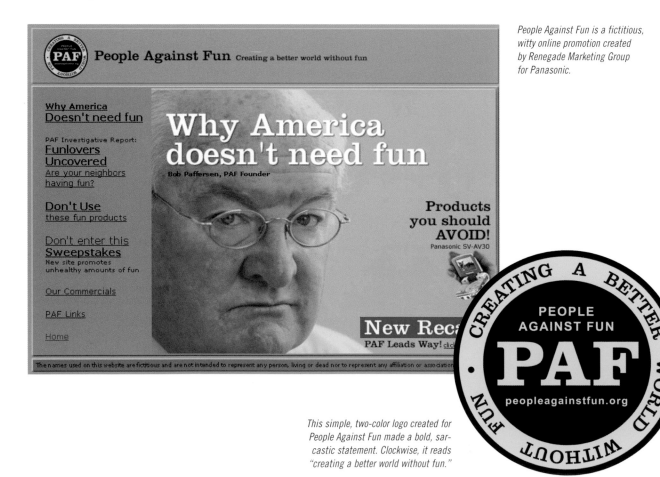

People Against Fun is a fictitious, witty online promotion created by Renegade Marketing Group for Panasonic.

This simple, two-color logo created for People Against Fun made a bold, sarcastic statement. Clockwise, it reads "creating a better world without fun."

Taking Risks

Then came the meeting where the idea had to be sold to the client. And believe it or not, there were actually people at Panasonic who thought that telling people not to buy your products was a bad sales strategy. So what finally convinced them? Well, as Drew Neisser, the president and CEO of Renegade explains, "Timing is everything. Our client had just attended a seminar on what makes teens tick. He was in the room and saw in People Against Fun what he had seen in the teen presentation: a counterculture to which he didn't much relate. He became an advocate for People Against Fun as a counterpoint to the more traditional fun site. Our client took the risk with us and helped to sell it into the rest of the company."

Once the site went live, the fictitious persona that was Bob Paffersen, chairman of People Against Fun, elicited a tremendous response—positive as well as negative. Generally speaking, the positive responses came from the site visitors that fell within the target demographic. In on the joke, they lauded People Against Fun for its "diligent dedication to the eradication of amusement and other recreational fun agents." Others expressed antipathy towards Paffersen and the "cause."

"Buzz" is difficult to measure, but it did not take long for the site to be the subject of news stories and several pages of Google results. Various elements of the site were designed to be viral, from Paffersen for office videos to the downloadable "Paffirmation," a guide to a life without fun. These and the URL for the site spread like wildfire. In the end, the site received millions of page views and far exceeded everyone's expectations. And we refuse to believe that it wiped out fun altogether.

The online promotion was created in response to a strategy stating that the Panasonic brand needed to be "coolified"—it needed to get males 18 to 24 years old to love the Panasonic brand.

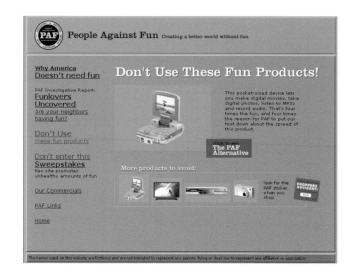

Believe it or not, there were actually people at Panasonic who thought that telling people not to buy your products was a bad sales strategy.

Research showed that the target appreciates and is more likely to identify with a brand that pokes fun at itself.

At this age, it's all about being cool. Really, what else is there? When you're a teenager, it doesn't seem to matter where in the world you live, what your income level is, or where you go to school. You share the same feelings of teens all over the world. You want to be seen as smart, hip, fun, and aware of the trends. You want to be liked, accepted. You want to belong to a club or a group, even if it's a group that's rebelling against all other groups. You want to fit in somewhere. Again, you want to be cool.

One way to be cool when you're a teen is to join a group of people who speak your language. Not just your native language, but your "teen" language—the language of your peers.

So Weiden + Kennedy teamed up with Plazm Media and created a poster campaign that ran for Nike—one that embraced adolescents' unique dialect.

"All cotton" is a basketball term. Those in the know know that it's a term for making a shot without hitting the backboard. So in teen talk, the All Cotton Club is where beat meets the street.

Design Firm	**Plazm Media**
Client	**Nike**
Project	**All Cotton Club Poster Series**

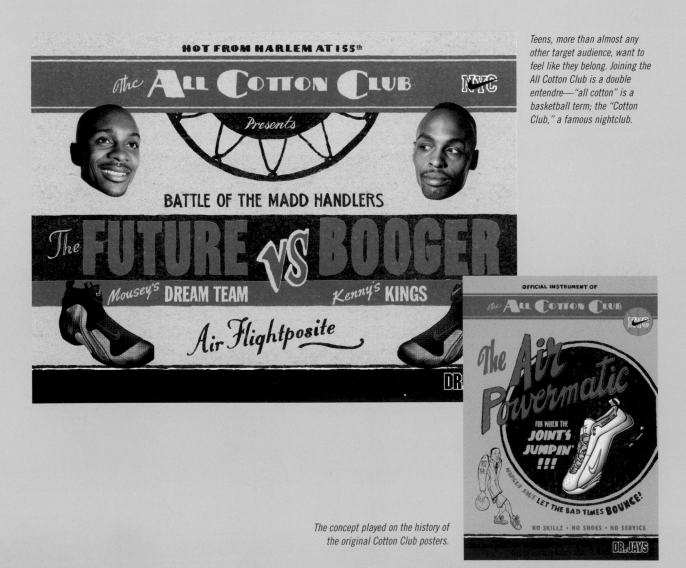

Teens, more than almost any other target audience, want to feel like they belong. Joining the All Cotton Club is a double entendre—"all cotton" is a basketball term; the "Cotton Club," a famous nightclub.

The concept played on the history of the original Cotton Club posters.

But at the same time, the Cotton Club conjures up images of the famous Harlem nightclub of the 1920s—the club whose clientele consisted of the wealthiest, most influential, and most notorious people around. Many of the early black entertainers got their start at the Cotton Club—Duke Ellington and Lena Horne, among others. So if you're *really* in the know, the All Cotton Club has many levels of meaning, embracing all things of interest to teenagers: sports, music, culture, clubs that exclude, clubs that include. (And just in case you're *not quite* in the know, the posters include plenty of other teen trigger words such as McNasty, Booger, Bad Times, and Boogie Nights.)

To make the promotion even more topical, the posters ran only in New York City, in the bus shelters and subways around the area where the original Cotton Club first opened its doors. It was what Nike and Weiden + Kennedy called a "City Attack" campaign—blanket a small area that has your core target audience and make it impossible to ignore. And the look of the posters was hand drawn, the way it was on the original Cotton Club posters.

Specifically, the posters were designed to promote the benefits of two new performance basketball shoes by Nike. The Air Powermatic is a basketball shoe specifically designed for power and an inside game, whereas the Air Flightposite shoe is designed for fitness and the outside game. But, much, much more important than that is the fact that the posters made teens feel like a part of something. They were a way to make teens feel cool.

The posters employ a mix of street ballers and professional New York basketball players.

Authenticity is very important to the design firm Plazm. It's a good thing, because savvy teens can spot inauthenticity a mile away.

Design Firm   Wasserman & Partners Advertising Inc.

Client   Vancouver Fringe

Project   Fringe Festival Posters

The Big Presentation Day

How do you think the following client meeting would go? The design team stands up to present the concepts. In one, there's a series of visuals where two men in karate uniforms break into a Rockettelike dance. In the second, a couple engages in Tantric sex only to have an elephant hand the woman a large knife. In the third, a young man demonstrates how to make balloon animals out of condoms.

Yes, condoms.

Well, the only thing you can say about client meetings is that you never know what to expect.

And "You never know what to expect" happens to be the tag line for the Vancouver Fringe Festival, which is what the aforementioned posters and ads were designed to promote. Since it is the Fringe Festival, after all, a bit of provocation is in order.

The Vancouver Fringe Festival has more than 100 performances in and around the Granville Island area. And as the tagline states so eloquently, "You never know what to expect."

The Main Event

The Vancouver Fringe Festival is a yearly event that features over a hundred different artistic performances. Browse through a program listing and one can see why it's a bit fringe. Performance titles like "Sketch Comedy for Dummies," "Sex, Violence, and the Meaning of Life" and "Sh*t Happens When You Party Naked" are the norm.

The festival had a lot of recognition in the local market, but little consistency in their messaging. People look forward to the festival every year, but in the past the events were stretched across the city, and thus a hassle to get to. In a bid to answer that issue, the festival relocated to Granville Island. But in doing that, they were in danger of alienating its core crowd, an artistic community, which had supported the event from its inception. Granville Island was more for tourists and West-siders.

The Contender Steps into the Ring

So Wasserman & Partners, a Canadian design firm, understood the challenge set forth to them: The work they produced had to have stopping power; it had to appeal to tourists and slightly more conservative folks, and yet it also had to remain true to its fringe element.

The concepts, once they got approved, were run as ads in Vancouver's urban weekly, placed in washroom stalls, and developed into T-shirts that were then sold at the Fringe Festival itself.

The birth of the idea came by accident. After a few weeks and reams of recycled paper, someone said one thing but the others thought he meant something else. Voila—an idea was born. That idea was to have someone show you how to do something a bit outrageous and then do a little bow at the end. The illustrations reinforce the concept because they're reminiscent of the safety instruction manuals you might find on airplanes.

This promotion took almost four months to complete. This process ended up being a bit complicated due to client inexperience, number of pieces, and number of people involved. Luckily, the design firm was able to overcome those problems "through diligence, sheer willpower, and pain."

Take a Bow

Back to that first infamous client meeting. Wasserman presented three creative platforms, but this project was the strong recommendation. As far as the sexual references are concerned, the client reacted perfectly. At first they were a little shocked, but inherently knew it was cool and it would appeal to their younger, core crowd. You know—the ones on the fringe.

The concept for the campaign was to have someone show the viewer how to do something outrageous and then end with a little bow.

Three different illustrators were used—Lorne Carnes, Jimmy Woo, and Alanna Cavanagh. The concepts fit together, however, because they are all "instructions with a twist."

Design Firm Squires & Company
Client James Bland
Project Promotional Mailer

The Essentials

Voodoo dolls. Test-tube beauty queens. A flesh-eating alligator about to meet its match by a scantily clad vixen. What would a promotional piece be without those things?

To say that photographer James Bland wanted to do something different when he called upon design firm Squires & Company to create a promotional mailer would be an understatement. There is nothing understated about the old pulp magazine covers re-created by the design firm and photographer. They are fun, funny, engaging, and sure to be noticed.

A Pretty Package

The mailer is an accordion-fold mailer of individually perforated cards, each measuring 4¼" x 6¼" (10.8 cm x 15.9 cm), and contained within a glassine envelope that also holds business cards and an info card. The elements were then enclosed between two pieces of cardboard, and packaging tape sealed the whole thing together. The piece was sent out to designers and art directors of agencies and magazines, with the hope that people would be intrigued enough to open it up and see what was inside. In fact, the entire piece was designed with the goal of preventing the "toss effect" at any step of the way.

Designers and art directors at agencies and magazines received this intriguing mail promotion from photographer James Bland.

Inside the glassine envelope is a variety of visual goodies.

Business and info cards complete the set.

The promotional piece came about when photographer James Bland—based in Dallas, Texas—wanted to show that he could create thematic photographs. The design firm presented several ideas, but none was as exciting as the idea to re-create old pulp magazine covers with actual models, sets, and customized typography.

Originally, the promotional piece was supposed to be mailed in just the glassine envelope, but the post office nixed that idea, stating that it would rip in mailing. But by that time, Squires & Company had already sealed the envelopes with the contents—all 2,500 of them. Brandon Murphy, creative director on the project, really wanted to keep the see-through envelope, so the design team sandwiched the envelopes between two pieces of cardboard and taped them together. They then rubber-stamped the outside with the return address and added type to convey more character. This process protected the contents and alluded to the roughened nature of the envelope's contents. It also added to the intrigue factor.

Achieving the Look

Amazingly enough, the only Photoshop manipulation used was on the *Mystery Science* image with the test-tube beauty. All the other models and backdrops were shot with a camera. The typography and the stressed look were added later via Adobe Illustrator and Photoshop. Even the logo has that retro sci-fi look.

Oh, yes, and the alligator *is* stuffed.

The promotion piece, designed by Squires & Company, has at its heart an accordion-folded set of perforated postcards, each painstakingly set up and shot by the photographer to re-create old pulp magazines.

Design Firm   Duffy Design (London)
Client   British Telecom
Project   British Telecom Book *A Complete Guide to Making Yourself 50% More Popular*

"I'm Popular or You're Fired"

British Telecom wanted to run a relatively straightforward promotion telling CEO's of major corporations that they could give their employees an opportunity to buy a PC for home use at a fraction of the normal price. Yet the end result is a laugh-out-loud book titled *A Complete Guide to Making Yourself 50% More Popular*. Within the foil stamped covers of fake leatherette are CEO bumper stickers, a banner to let employees know that you offer them free water daily, and pithy sayings you can adopt such as "I'm popular or you're fired." The kicker, of course, is that while all of those ways might help to make a CEO more popular, nothing really does it like offering employees reasonably priced computers for their home.

Believe it or not, the idea to create such a book was arrived at very quickly. When sitting around, discussing the promotion, there was an adamant belief that the British Telecom promotion *would*, in fact, make CEO's more popular with their employees. As soon as the initial idea jelled, it took about four days to create the prototype, which looked almost exactly like the final version. As Tim Watson of Duffy Design notes, "Once we had the overall idea, each page was a joy to create." It then took approximately four months to produce the whole book and get it printed.

Tim Watson of Duffy Design notes, it appears to be a "free Christmas desk diary—the sort of gift you get sent by some obscure supplier who has produced these things for 20 years and is under the misunderstanding that everyone loves them."

These bumper stickers are guaranteed to increase any CEO's popularity by 50 percent.

The Gift That Nobody Wants

The details are all well thought to make the piece look very tongue in cheek and over the top. The idea for the look of the piece was to make it appear to be a "free Christmas desk diary—the sort of gift you get sent by some obscure supplier who has produced these things for 20 years and is under the misunderstanding that everyone loves them," notes Tim, drolly.

The entire piece ended up being more than 100 pages long. The idea was to have it feel "slightly lavish, but in a naff sort of way." This was done through the use of bold colors and foldouts with interactive pieces such as stickers. The piece ended up being nine colors throughout. The paper stock took a bit of experimentation in the proofing stage. The design team finally chose a G.F. Smith paper stock called Zen because the definition of the shots appeared to be the best against it, and they thought a more traditional feel to the stock would be most appropriate. The most difficult part of production, perhaps surprisingly, was to find a sticker backing stock that could be printed on the reverse side. Most sticker stocks, it turns out, have a repeated print of the brand name on the back. But dilemmas such as that aside, the overall production process went quite smoothly, and the books were hand delivered to the CEO's of the top 100 companies in the United Kingdom.

Although it's too early to tell actual results, we're quite sure there are many newly popular CEO's in the British Empire.

The details are all well thought out, making the book very tongue in cheek and over the top.

While CEO's can learn how to become more popular with this handbook, nothing really does it like offering employees reasonably priced computers for their home.

Design Firm | Nolin Branding and Design
Client | Domtar
Project | Boring Paper Promotion

Two Different Audiences, Two Different Approaches

Every communication piece a company creates says something about their business. And ideally, every piece should complement the others. The best way to ensure that this consistently happens? Being honest and straightforward with all of your audiences all of the time. The design firm Nolin, and their client, Domtar, a paper producer, executed a textbook example of this with two very different pieces to two very different audiences.

How Many Clients Would Be Willing to Admit Their Product Was Boring?

For a new Domtar trade show brochure, it was determined that the main goal should be to communicate the company's distinctive personality and capture the essence of their new tagline: Domtar. A different feel. The company is proud that their employees are fun to do business with and don't take themselves too seriously. After all, they deal with paper—a plain, flat substance that just doesn't do too much. A substance that is, in a word, boring.

Nolin creative director Barbara Jacques explains, "We wanted to show that paper needs people. Paper needs inspiration, creativity, and feelings." From this directive, the "boring" brochure was born. It's a good-humored, visual piece that comes right out and admits that paper is indeed boring, but in the process succeeds in screaming that Domtar people most certainly are not.

boring

The Boring brochure maintained a clear and simple look, featuring colorful typography and large images. This clean design allows the audience to recognize that the paper is a vital part of the layout.

Nolin creative director Barbara Jacques explains, "We wanted to show that paper needs people. Paper needs inspiration, creativity, and feelings."

Although their products might be boring, the people at Domtar certainly are not—just take a look at their brochure.

Met with almost instant approval, this concept was the only one ever developed. The final brochure was received extremely well by both Domtar clients and employees. For the record, our sources tell us that not one person claimed that Domtar was boring.

The Canvas May Be Boring. The Results Are Not.

When it was time to create the Domtar annual report, Nolin and the client understood that this piece would be talking to an entirely different audience. One that may not appreciate the "boring" message as much as the trade show set. The annual report would go out to investors, shareholders, and company employees. In an effort to keep what could have been a stodgy piece out of the recycling bin, the agency and client decided to take a step away from the ingrained perception of the pulp and paper industry as being old-fashioned, straightforward, and well, boring.

The idea was to position Domtar as a dynamic and contemporary company, a leader in the industry. Jacques explains, "In spite of a very tight timetable, we knew immediately that we were on the same wavelength. We had hit on the perfect concept: Pulling together . . . we planned on the symbolism of the forest, identifying it with team spirt and creativity." Not to mention trees and paper. Like the Boring campaign before it, the annual report presented an honest view of Domtar.

Designers employed bold and modern colors to bring the piece to life, and the team made an effort to highlight the company's vision for the upcoming three years.

From briefing to delivery, the entire project took less than three months. Jacques confirms, "Everything went well at every step." And along with honesty, quality, and a sense of humor, what more could you want from your paper company?

The company's annual report went out to investors, shareholders, and company employees, and it positioned Domtar as a dynamic and contemporary company, a leader in the industry.

Using an insert—something not often seen in run-of-the-mill annual reports—the piece clearly states company objectives and their overall commitment to quality. The client would eventually print more inserts to distribute among the employees.

Rock, Scissors, Paper, Shoot!

Rock

The Hard Rock Café—the perfect place for a party when you really want things to rock!

From this location a promotion evolved to invite people to this event and get them excited by it. How excited? The promotion shows seven different "rock moves" they can learn to do that will essentially "guarantee rock stardom." Created by Kolegram in Ottawa, Canada, the promotion had as its mantra: "We believe a rocking attitude is what makes things happen."

Paper

The client is Buntin Reid, a paper distributor. They often organize events to show off their new and existing products. The event they organized was a paper show, but a hard-rockin', fun-lovin' paper show. The promotion, printed on paper, naturally, was a cyan-magenta-yellow-black (CMYK) flyer that opens up to be a 19½" x 27½" (49.5 cm x 70 cm) poster. It was printed on Luna Matte 100-pound text, and it was shrink wrapped to be sent out in the mail. The piece was sent to graphic designers, agencies, and people working in the communications industry.

But what makes this promotion remarkable is the fact that you actually want to read it! The content and pictures are fun and amusing—a sure-fire recipe to encourage readers to keep reading and maybe even save it or at least look at it more than once. This is especially important since the target audience is a very design-savvy group of graphic designers, project managers, printers, and other paper customers from the Ottawa region.

Who wouldn't want to attend a hard-rocking party for a paper show after seeing this humorous and engaging promotion?

Scissors

As for problems encountered in the production process, there were only three—budget, budget, and budget. The budget meant things just had to be cut, and the designers had to live with it. The original strategy was to have a saddle-stitched booklet with the content inside, and the full-sized poster folded and glued in the inside back cover. Unfortunately that feature had to be cut because of budget. The piece also had to be resized many times due to the changing budgets, and at one point the design firm had to switch printers.

Shoot!

Creative director Mike Teixeira directed the promotion. He put on the rock star outfit and posed for photographs (the fact that he played in a rock band himself definitely helped). He knew he could do the rock star moves and wanted everything to be exaggerated and grand. Teixeira describes the shoot: "I had a blast at the photo shoot. The photographer and I laughed so much. We did the photos in a few hours, right after some department store's shoot, using the same white background. It worked!"

And the Winner Is . . .

In the end, everything worked out great. The paper show was a hit. The promotion really got people in the rock and roll mood. There were life-sized banners of all the moves hanging inside the Hard Rock Café. Kolegram knew the promotion had to be energetic and humorous if they expected people to show up, and that's exactly what happened. Rock on!

Due to budget constraints, Mike Teixeira, the creative director of the piece, donned the rock-star outfit. His over-the-top moves make this piece hysterical and memorable.

"Graze on some excellent grub, see the latest cool papers, win prizes, and check out the cool guitars on the wall." Whether you're into rock and roll or papers, this party had it all.

Design Firm Hornall Anderson Design Works
Client Erickson McGovern
Project 30th Anniversary Promotional Announcement

A Numbers Game

The number 30. Not as interesting as some numbers. There's nothing superstitious about it. It's not a prime number, a dozen, a hundred. It's not the number of cards in a deck, or pennies in a quarter, or days in a week. As lackluster as it might seem, however, Hornall Anderson Design Works managed to elevate the number 30 to a whole new level. Although most people may choose to hide their age after they reach 29, Hornall Anderson Design Works decided to go to the opposite extreme. Instead, they dared to ask: Why hide your age when you can flaunt it?

Therein lies the beauty of the idea. For the thirtieth birthday of their client, the architectural firm Erickson McGovern, Hornall Anderson decided to do an entire concept based around the number 30. One of the most unusual invitations one could ever hope to receive, the final result is a stack of cards encased in a small cardboard box that all contain the number 30 in a humorous and witty, and thus extremely memorable, fashion.

All the cards contained in the small cardboard box had some visual connection to the number 30, which referenced the 30-year anniversary of architectural firm Erickson McGovern.

To produce the piece as efficiently as possible, design firm Hornall Anderson had to figure out how to end up with 28 paper cards and a box container. So they worked backwards and divided out the space on two 12" x 18" (30.5 cm x 46 cm) press sheets. The remaining two cards were engraved metal.

Some cards had interesting facts about the history of Erickson McGovern and its relationship to the culture.

Turning 30 Has Never Been More Fun

The cards are the size of ordinary business cards, with the first card in each box made out of engraved metal. Distributed to the company's clients, friends, and employees, the first metal card simply invited the recipient of said box to Erickson McGovern's thirtieth anniversary reception. But it's in the remaining 29 cards where the fun lies. These cards poke fun at people, events, and the history of the firm, with cards containing quips such as, "He always gave at least 30%," "30/30 Hindsight" and "30 years ago I never thought . . ." The quirky sayings are combined with equally quirky artwork that consists of graphic treatments, clip art, black-and-white photos of the partners in the firm, and four-color stock photography. Several of the cards give insight into the firm's history, digging deep into the starting days 30 years prior. A favorite example: A color photo of a supermarket shelf with shrink-wrapped packages of meat has the words "in 1972" superimposed. On the back side is the punchline, "We bartered meat in exchange for service." Or, this fact, also from 1972 (which sounds like a rough year for the firm) "on 9:29:1972 we made a profit of $30!" The piece was designed so that the recipient typically doesn't get the number 30 reference until about halfway through reviewing the stack. The fact that they have to figure out the concept makes it more rewarding.

The final piece is a keepsake that the recipients are bound to hold on to, which not only sets the tone for a great celebration, but commemorates the colorful history of the firm with wit, grace, and honesty. In looking back on the past 30 years of the company in such a fashion, people can also look forward to the future years of the company with excitement.

The number 30 could not be reached for comment.

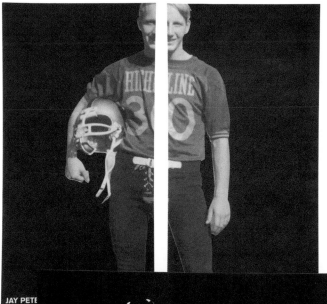

Some cards simply had witty sayings about the number 30 itself. A bit of advice about not trusting anyone under 30 becomes especially apropos now that the firm has finally reached that landmark age.

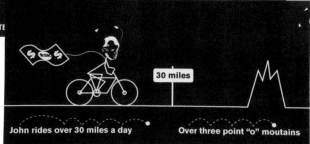

Some of the cards had photos or other interesting tidbits about the partners in the firm and always related back to the number 30.

Design Firm **Duffy Design (Minneapolis)**

Client **Archipelago (ARCA)**

Project **Direct Mail Campaign**

We could introduce this next promotion by using some clever, unexpected hook to draw you in. Then, we could ramble on for a bit about joke and gimmick shops—maybe even propose a new theory or two on the educational value of toys. This segment certainly has the potential to develop into a very interesting preamble. But there will be none of that. Because, as you'll see, this next promotion does just that: It captures the audience's attention right from the start and makes them want to read on and learn more. And it does it so well that there's really no point for us to try.

Turning a Potentially Boring Assignment . . .

So, imagine your ad agency or design firm has just been called on to develop a promotional direct-mailer campaign for a stock exchange. Your initial thought might be, "A financial account! This is just going to be *loads* of fun." And quite understandably so. Well, Duffy Design, a company of Fallon Worldwide, was the lucky design firm assigned to the job. And this project was loads of fun.

Their client was Archipelago (ARCA), an electronic stock exchange that competes with NASDAQ, NYSE, and ASE, as well as alternative trading systems. Before the new campaign, ARCA was primarily trading NASDAQ volume. So, in short, the goal was to expand into the NYSE, an unrealized territory.

Prime campaign targets included both current and prospective Archipelago traders. Jennifer Jagielski of Duffy describes what these people are all about: "[They] are work-hard, play-hard guys with short attention spans and little time to pay attention to advertising messages." And, with that in mind, the creative team developed a whole line of toys—er, marketing tools.

Want to remain anonymous? Then put on this mask—and learn about trader anonymity.

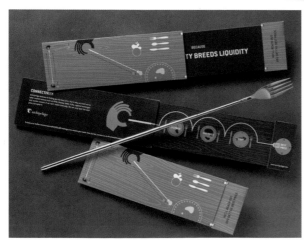

The connectivity fork is a piece all about how Archipelago reaches out and finds the best prices for its customers.

The Electronic Naturals sing about the benefits of electronic trading.

. . . Into a Fun One

Each direct-mail piece was essentially a different gag—and each carried a unique selling point. Jagielski explains, "Each piece played off a different 'weakness' of the NYSE, and leveraged ARCA's strengths." One mailer, for instance, was a mysterious blue envelope. Pull a tab, and out came a telescoping fork. This piece, as the copy on the packaging explained, was all about connectivity; it represented Archipelago's ability to reach out and find the best prices for its customers.

In another example, one piece in the campaign was a cardboard cutout of a face wearing a Groucho Marx–esque disguise—complete with a fake nose and moustache. The header on the back read, "Put on a mask," and below that was a nametag that said, "Hello, my name is Anyone." This particular piece highlighted yet another one of Archipelago's strengths: their ability to preserve trader anonymity.

In the end, the client was very pleased with Duffy's work; the campaign, they reported, generated a lot of positive talk and email messages among their target audience. And the folks at Duffy must have been thrilled, too—their campaign was an easy sell to the client, as outlandish as it was. Jagielski says, "[Archipelago] are willing to take risks and communicate in an unexpected way . . . and they were very helpful in explaining many of the 'industry inside' hot buttons and language to make our pieces really strong."

No More Joking Around

Okay, we gypped you out of a decent intro. So, in a few words, we'll sum up the moral of the story for you: If you're looking for an easy career in advertising or design, make sure all your clients are as receptive to bold and wacky ideas as Archipelago. Alternatively, consider this: Unexpectedness is a definite attention grabber.

Remember the buzzing handshake? This is to remind traders that there is always open access when trading with Archipelago.

Unlike Miss Princess Fun Brick here, Archipelago believes in promoting and maintaining a competitive environment.

Archipelago's lightning-fast electronic trading system means you'll never find yourself trading at the speed of this guy.

Unexpected

Surprise! The promotions in this section make one's eyes widen. No matter what the category, target audience, or format is, an unexpected promotion is one that is sure to make someone say "Wow, I wish I had thought of that!"

Design Firm   **Templin Brink Design**
Client   **Target**
Project   **Michael Graves Design Collection Promotion**

Imagine coming up with an idea for a promotion. You're sitting around, brainstorming with another designer, and one of you says, "How 'bout we do a pop-up ad insert?"

Blood, Sweat, and Tears

Fast forward a month. Twenty-one 13-person teams are working eight-hour shifts for four weeks to make your promotional idea happen. And that doesn't even include the Web and sheet-fed print portion of the job—that's just the folding part, the part of the process that needs the actual "popping up." A bit mind-boggling—just think about it—13 people had to touch each and every part of your promotional piece to make it happen.

But then again, the promotion was for Target, a company that "merely" sells good quality merchandise at low prices, but has a brand that transcends that, a brand that is mod, trendy, bold, hip. Declared by a recent USA Today poll as "in," Target is *the* place to find the latest trends at the best prices.

Templin Brink, a San Francisco design agency, was assigned a specific promotional project for Target. The strategy behind this promotion was to reinvigorate the Michael Graves Design Collection, a collection of products sold exclusively at Target. The Michael Graves brand had been around for a few years and the impetus was to get people jazzed again about this incredible line of products.

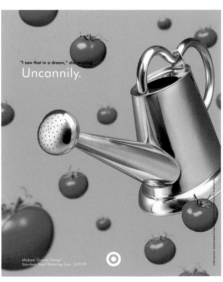 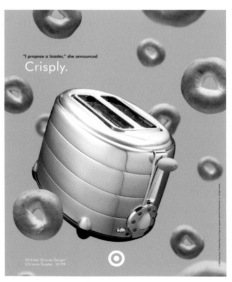 

The target audience is primarily women in the 25- to 44-year-old age group. Joel Templin, creative director, notes: "I think the campaign, like any Target campaign, is appealing because it's fun and has bold energy."

Everything Works Together

The promotional campaign was fairly extensive, involving the creation of a print ad campaign, direct mail (that was sent out to a list of Target's Graves shoppers), a press kit, and other innovative PR and marketing ideas. And what Templin Brink did so well was to conceptualize and execute all the various components into a seamless campaign, one that gave the Michael Graves Design Collection a fresh, updated feeling while still staying true to the core Target brand.

Templin Brink Design has an agency philosophy of linking together a brand's history and destiny together. A perfect philosophy in a case like this. Target has a bold and colorful history and seems destined for continued success—it was started in 1962 in Roseville, Minnesota, and has since grown to 1,107 stores across the United States.

Sometimes the Best Ideas Just Pop Up

The campaign has been extremely successful in capturing people's imagination and creating brand awareness. Templin Brink is currently on their third year of the campaign. Part of the assignment is always coming up with extra credit ideas, events, or unusual ways to promote the collection. This year the Michael Graves Design Collection included freestanding pavilions that would be offered only at Target.com. So, in a typical creative brainstorming session, the design team attempted to create an innovative promotional idea that would showcase those pavilions. And one designer says to the other, "Hey, how 'bout we do a pop-up insert?"

And the rest, as we know, is history.

The press kit went along with the other materials to create a seamless, visually vibrant campaign.

The infamous ad insert was "incredibly complex to produce from a paper-engineering standpoint taking twenty-one teams of thirteen people each working eight-hour shifts for four weeks to put it together."

Design Firm **Plazm Media**
Client **Portland Institute for Contemporary Art**
Project **Pink Posters**

Artistic Expression

Severed body parts. It's hard not to be provocative when designing posters using actual body parts. Add to that the word "severed," and it's nigh impossible. Of course, being provocative is just what Plazm Media set out to be when they designed a series of posters for the Portland Institute of Contemporary Art (PICA).

First, just for the record, the body parts were already severed when they were photographed. No magic of Photoshop was used here. The photographer, Christian Witkin, had a difficult time finding available body parts to photograph, as one might expect. But then, art has always been about dogged determination.

Art in the Public Sphere

The purpose of the posters was twofold. On one hand, they were designed to promote Portland's Contemporary Art Museum and raise awareness of it. But they were also designed to attract people to an exhibition called "Counter Canvas," which is all about art in the public sphere. And what better way to promote art in the public sphere than to create art in the public sphere that gets noticed and talked about?

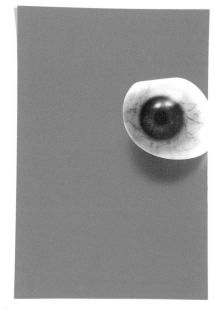

The posters were a visual metaphor. Each one represented one of the five senses, this one being touch, with the Portland Institute of Contemporary Art becoming the sixth sense.

The actual printing was a combination of litho and silk screen. The body parts were printed litho as a tritone using silver and two blacks. The pink is a silkscreen trapped to the image. The image shadow overprints.

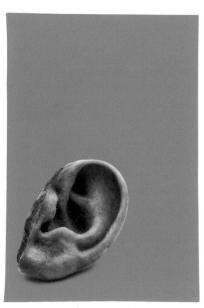

One can only wonder what was served for lunch at the photo shoot where severed body parts were photographed.

Around 1,000 posters were printed and wild posted around the streets of Portland, Oregon.

Joshua Berger of Plazm Media likes to give credit where credit is due. According to him, the real inspiration for the idea came from PICA itself, who has a willingness to raise questions yet respect the audience's intelligence to reach their own conclusions. The art museum strives to embrace the unknown, to push people in the direction of a more open mind. Even when a more open mind means approval of a layout that shows severed body parts on hot pink backgrounds.

Berger, who collaborated on the posters with creative director John Jay, becomes animated when he speaks of the project. "The very color itself elicits political, sexual, and gender overtones. Combined with a severed finger, ear, tongue, eyeball, or nose, the hope was to create a new provocation in the street. The purpose of these icons of the human senses was to ignite the first step of the creative process, the spontaneous act of thinking. Rarely does one consider the act of provocation through elegance. To beautifully lull one into danger . . . into the gallery of PICA."

The Work on Display

The posters went up one at a time over a six-week period and were posted on construction walls and any surface legally available. There was no copy, only a logo on the last poster to go up. People were left to figure out the puzzle by piecing together the five senses—an eye, an ear, a nose, a tongue, a finger—with PICA metaphorically becoming the sixth sense. Along with the posters, small 2" x 3" (5.1 cm x 7.6 cm) cards were also produced using the images. PICA and Plazm staff got cards each week and were asked to surreptitiously hand them out and leave them in public places. They were also mailed—one a week for six weeks—in unmarked envelopes from the central post office to various media sources.

As for the reaction—like the best art, the posters evoked extreme reactions in people. Love 'em or hate 'em, they did get a response. Many posters were defaced and others were appropriated by other artists. In the gallery, PICA had an entire wall painted pink with each poster mounted across the length of the wall. And, true to form, someone actually tagged the gallery wall itself.

All That Matters in the End

The client, on the other hand, was very pleased. They have since been seen using pink for other promotions.

The only copy appeared on this final poster with the logo, which went up during the last week of the six-week blitz.

Once viewers were "seductively lulled into the gallery through provocation," there was an area of the exhibit that had a bright pink wall where all the posters were displayed.

It's not easy being on the brink of adulthood. You might have just completed college, or have been working for a couple of years. You are suddenly responsible for more things than you ever thought possible. Perhaps you are just buying your first car, or even buying your first house. Maybe you're thinking of getting married. But one thing is for sure—you don't want to give up on the fun stuff. Some days, you still have the urge to be a kid. Some days, you just don't want to be old.

Designers and marketers targeting this age group need to be aware of this duality. This age group knows it needs to make certain decisions responsibly. So it's a group that seeks out more information about certain products and services than it used to.

But at the same time, members of this age group lead incredibly busy lifestyles. So brand names mean something because they are the ultimate time-saver. Yet unlike the younger demographic, they no longer use brand names to be a part of the club.

Design Firm   **Sandstrom Design**
Client   **The State of Oregon (USA)**
Project   **X-Pack Smoking Cessation Program**

DESIGNS THAT STAND UP SPEAK OUT AND CANT BE IGNORED

The X-Pack is a self-help smoking cessation kit, packaged in a way that is attractive to the target audience— young adults aged 20–26.

And one other thing to remember—you can't talk to them like they're not still hip. After all, young adults still want to have fun.

Sandstrom Design needed to talk to this age group with an incredibly challenging project—to get young adults in the state of Oregon to stop smoking. Research confirmed the conflicting stresses of this target: they had started smoking in their more carefree days and now were beginning to regret their decision. They needed help, but help came with a caveat. It needed to be fun, also.

Enter the X-Pack. A self-help smoking cessation kit, packaged in a way that is attractive to the target audience, with a mix of quick, simple information along with fun things to do instead of smoking.

Among the components: a youth-oriented smoking cessation guide complete with a quit plan and quit day checklist; motivational messages; testimonials of successful quit attempts by peers; information on nicotine replacement therapy. And, of course, the fun stuff: various products to keep the hand and mouth busy during the quitting process (gum, cinnamon toothpicks, stress putty); and an incentive for registering the product (a Borders Books and Music gift certificate). All materials were based on the best medical practice, combining insights from both adult and adolescent smoking cessation research.

And everything was packaged in a way that said "we know you are still hip."

Among the components: a youth-oriented smoking cessation guide complete with a quit plan and quit day checklist; motivational messages and, of course, the fun stuff—gum, cinnamon toothpicks, and stress putty.

The goal of this project was to get young adults in the state of Oregon to stop smoking through an informative, yet fun, approach.

Design Firm Amoeba Corp.
Client Jill and Steven Miller
Project Wedding Invitation

A wedding. A time of great tradition. Stuffy, scripty invitations on plain cream stock are not usually seen in a book on promotions. But this was a wedding that was promoted in a most unusual way.

An Untraditional Announcement

Jill Furnival and Stephen Miller, a happy couple about to be married, wanted an invitation that was different from anything they had seen before and that would leave a lasting impression on their guests. The couple contacted Michael Kelar of Amoeba Corp. because they were aware of his design work as well as his personal artwork. The creative brief was pretty brief (excuse the pun); Michael was given a blank canvas—a designer's dream. He sold the couple on an idea to create an invitation package that would be "an eclectic mix of vintage/modern elements that would take the viewer through a dynamic visual story rather than just displaying the simple facts." It was a form of anti-design—invitees would have to work for the information rather than have it presented to them in a straightforward fashion. The concept for the invitation was a reflection of the couple's personalities and eclectic tastes, much like the actual wedding event itself. The concept was to create a package that had many formal aspects but was not traditional in its content. The project took a little more than two months from concept to completion.

MICHAEL KELAR
6-1061 BRAEMAR AVE.
TORONTO, ONTARIO

From the moment the guests received the envelope in the mail, they could guess this was not a traditional wedding invitation. And they were not disappointed.

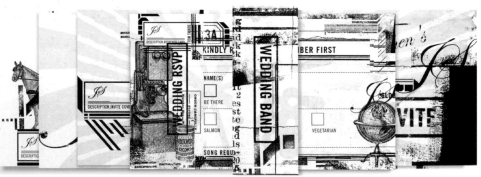

The concept for the invitation was "an eclectic mix of vintage/modern elements that would take the viewer through a dynamic visual stay."

Adding a Personal Touch

The production process was as unconventional as the invitation itself. Due to a limited budget, the 150 wedding invitations and associated collateral were hand assembled. From hand litho mounting 1960s vintage wallpaper to each invitation card to trimming and assembly, the entire production process took more than two weeks to complete. Four sets of skilled hands, many long nights, and a lot of take-out was needed to accomplish such a feat—a true example of limited edition in the world of art and design.

Kelar notes that the most interesting part of the project was the attention to detail—each piece that was created for the wedding was highly customized and unique. Graphic elements, textures, typography, and the vintage etchings were never duplicated throughout the entire package—every element was customized and hand manipulated to emphasize the unique qualities of the couple's personalities and their wedding party.

Another interesting note was that few guests actually returned the RSVP card and instead kept the entire invitation package. But luckily they did show up!

A Happy Couple

There are lots of things to be nervous about when planning a wedding, including the presentation of concepts to the bride- and groom-to-be. When they first saw the design, the couple reacted exactly like clients who see something truly unusual. They gasped, took a few minutes to recover, and then joked about whether anyone would show up. They had asked for something different, and different is what they got. And when all of the pieces were designed and the full package was presented as one cohesive idea, the couple saw the method in the madness. The wedding was a huge success and the invitations were the subject of many conversations. And the couple is still very happily married.

The design theme was carried through to the celebration, with menus, gift CDs, and thank-you notes included in the cohesive theme.

Many of the guests liked the package so much that they were reluctant to send back the RSVP card and destroy the integrity of the package.

Design Firm   **Emery Vincent Design**
Client   **Emery Vincent Design**
Project   **September 11th Anniversary Posters**

Designers Unite

It was a year after the September 11th tragedy. The people of New York City and Washington were remembering what happened. It was an event that shocked the world. So is it surprising that halfway across the globe, in Sydney, Australia, people were remembering, too? As Sharon Nixon of Emery Vincent Design states, "Everyone was touched by the tragedy in some way whether through clients, the extensive media coverage, or the loss of friends—the effects were global."

Strategy and Execution

So Emery Vincent Design decided to take action by creating a series of posters that would mark the anniversary. The office as a whole became involved in the project. The design firm felt that a visible public response, in a medium that has been typically used for expression—the street poster—was an appropriate vehicle. The thinking was that the posters would be partly about giving the studio an opportunity to express its reaction to this significant world event, but also would share this anonymously with the wider community as a catalyst for debate. The posters were designed to be an urban statement that came from the street. They were placed on telegraph poles along a busy inner-city street in a guerilla-style campaign. The street posters in their own right are subversive. There was a guerilla tactic in putting them up in Sydney where there is a policy of no street pole posters—and yet there are many. The posters were placed anonymously; there was no reference to Emery Vincent Design. The idea was to make a social comment and spark community debate.

Posters commemorating the anniversary of September 11th were placed on telegraph poles along busy inner-city streets in Sydney, Australia, in a guerilla-style campaign.

Their tactics were somewhat subversive because in Sydney there is a policy of no street pole posters—and yet there are many.

So all along the roads in inner urban Sydney—areas with different demographics and psychographics—the posters were placed. Emery Vincent consciously chose a variety of communities to try to spark a variety of personal responses.

The Message and Content

The posters were part of a studio project, which generated 15 designs. The studio collectively selected three designs to be produced. Everyone was uniquely affected by the tragedy and responded in a different manner ranging from graphically aggressive, political, and antiterrorist to compassionate and peaceful expressions. Each of the three posters that were chosen promoted and represented one of three common themes—commemoration for those who died; compassion, and the need to pursue peace; and a political commentary on America's stand on terrorism.

The posters were restricted to a two-color palette and a limited screen-printed edition. The stark use of red, black, and white adds to the impact of the design. And as for the response, Sharon Nixon simply states, "Public reaction is difficult to gauge as the lifespan of these posters is generally short and often undocumented. Hopefully, for the instant they are up, there is engagement, review, and a personal response."

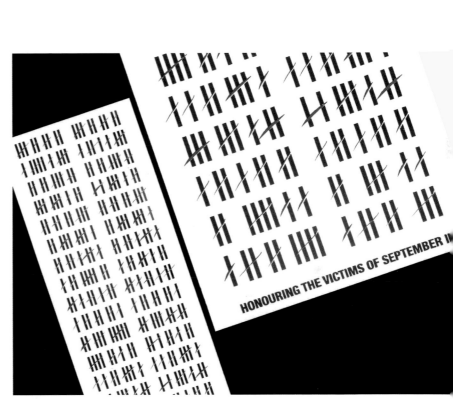

Public reaction was difficult to gauge due to the lifespan of these posters, which is generally short and often undocumented. One can hope that these designs caused engagement, review, and a personal response.

Everyone was uniquely affected by the tragedy and responded in a different manner ranging from graphically aggressive, political, and antiterrorist to compassionate and peaceful expressions.

The lowly business card. How great of a promotional vehicle can it be?

In the case of Howalt Design, the answer is: "Quite great indeed."

A Solo Project

Paul Howalt runs his own illustration studio. He doesn't have a large budget to advertise himself as an illustrator simply because illustrator's fees don't justify it. So he knew he had to come up with a simple, yet out-of-the-ordinary way to get a fairly large taste of the flavor and style of his work in front of art directors as conveniently as possible. He had specific criteria in mind: It had to be easy to mail and store, and it had to show a lot of work. So instead of sinking most of his budget into hit-or-miss periodic mailings, he decided to invest in an item that served multiple objectives and stood out from the sea of competitor's postcards.

The idea for the business card came out of his personal philosophy about design. Howalt states, "I'd have to say I'm a very visually stimulated human being. I understand how an overwhelmingly large body of good work affects me when I see it, so I tend to try and go a bit overboard when selling myself to art directors and creative directors, whom I assume tend to respond along the same lines. I believe that you can't communicate anything until you have someone's attention. When doing work I always ask myself if the piece is going to grab viewers by the eye sockets."

And grab viewers by the eye sockets this does. At first glance, it looks like an ordinary business card, albeit a thick one. But upon closer examination, the card springs open to reveal a glossy, four-color accordion-fold insert of Howalt's work. One is reminded of those old cartoons where, when surprised, a character's eyes would pop out of its head, held on by, er, yes, springs.

When illustrator Paul Howalt needed to promote himself, he designed a business card that literally sprang to life when opened.

Putting It All Together

Howalt is glad it works, because it does take a certain bit of assembly on his part before it can get into the appropriate people's hands. "The hard part is mustering the discipline to glue and fold a bunch of these each week to mail and pass out. The die-cut notch was a simple drill job and the scores are parallel; I tried to keep it simple for budget level printers."

Once the idea for the card sprang to life, the actual execution was easy. The illustrations were simply taken from past work; the rest of it was completed in about a day. The one problem Paul noticed was that it was hard to stop working on it, simply because, as he says "I tend to be such a harsh critic when doing work for myself as a client."

A Good Leave-Behind

As a final interesting note, at design and illustration conferences, Paul has left the cards lying around so those who find them might perceive them as something dropped from an art director's business card file. When he checks on the cards minutes later, they are always gone. Perhaps they can be found along with the art director's empty eye sockets.

Each of the 1,000 cards printed ended up costing about 75 cents.

The printing of the card was uncomplicated—it was a simple work and turn on both pieces.

Lush

There's a certain indescribable richness about a promotion that's designed to be lush. Regardless of what the actual budget is, the person receiving the promotion feels as if no expense has been spared. It is evident in every little detail: maybe it's the weight of the paper, a precious piece of typography, a stunning photograph, or deep, opulent colors. The end result is something that can be treasured long after the promotion is over.

Design Firm **Riordon Design**
Client **Riordon Design**
Project **Personal Calendar**

"365 new mornings. 8,760 hours to spend. 525,600 passing moments. One full circle of time."

The Day That Never Ends

And so begins one of the more poetic promotions to be found, a lowly personal calendar, elevated to new heights through design, poetic writing, and a most unusual production technique.

Every year Riordon designs a custom gift to give to their existing client base and prospects. For 2004, it was a personal calendar, measuring 6½" x 8½" (16.5 cm x 21.6 cm), featuring simulated velvet pastel blue book covers with silver foil stamping. Sandwiched in between the covers is a two-color accordion calendar insert and, holding it together, a wide rubber band with the pi symbol imprinted on it.

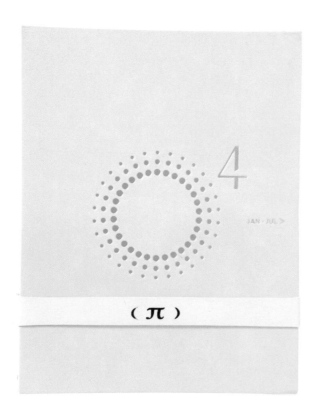

When Riordon sets out to design each year's custom gift piece, part of the criteria is to design something that showcases the design firm's capability in presentation design—something memorable, something that people will keep around and not be quick to discard.

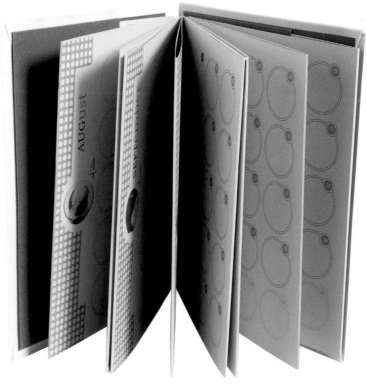

The designers at Riordon find projects like this personal calendar fun to do. It's the kind of project that not only showcases the imaginations and skills of the design team, but it's essential for internal morale building.

Half-Time

One thing that makes this piece unique is that the year is split in the middle. The first six months of this calendar book start at the front cover and go to the middle. For the second half of the year, the user flips the book over, and starts all over from the back cover. This not only complements the circular theme, but was a clever solution to a production quandary. As Ric Riordon, design firm founder, explains: "We wanted to create a continuous linear layout of the calendar year and the only way to achieve this on one sheet of stock was to set it up in this fashion."

The theme of the personal calendar is a playful yet philosophical look at the concept of infinity and the circle. According to Riordon, using the mathematical formula pi and its "interwoven presence in all the designed universe, the implied association is made that infinity, or eternity, exists in tandem with all matter and our measurement of time." Lest one think that is too esoteric, keep in mind that the piece was designed to appeal to a target audience consisting mostly of smart corporate professionals and entrepreneurs.

Timing Is Everything

Ironically enough, the biggest problem in producing a piece like this was the timing. The assembly of the piece was more intense than first anticipated. The various elements were produced by three different vendors, and then the 400 books were assembled and wrapped at the studio. The book covers were late. The die line for the insert calendar was off, which required hand trimming with an X-acto blade in order to slip them into the covers. The bands weren't perfect when they arrived. Some had messy printing; others were a little tight on the finished book. So everyone had to sort through the bands and do a quality purge. Fortunately, there were plenty of extras.

We hope that the first entry into Riordan's new personal calendar is an early starting date for next year's promotion.

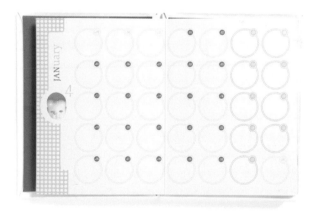

Beyond being creative, the goals of the piece were that it "needed to showcase intelligence, serve a function, and fulfill a purpose," notes Ric Riordon, founder of the design firm. The following quotation from Jonathan Swift highlights this perfectly: "I'm up and down and round about yet the world can't find me out; though hundreds have employed their leisure, they never yet could find my measure."

Design Firm **Anvil Graphic Design, Inc.**
Client **Anvil Graphic Design, Inc.**
Project **Gift Wrap**

Have you ever thought about the creative process that goes into creating gift wrap?

Do you imagine it to be an easy process, one that simply involves designing a single pattern that can be repeated over and over on a large roll of paper?

Did you ever think that each design might have to be critiqued in numerous formal presentation scenarios and go through many rounds of revisions, until a team of designers feels it works?

Well, this is the real story . . .

A Gift for You

Granted, this is not just any gift wrap—it is gift wrap that is designed to be used as a promotional tool for Anvil Graphic Design, a design firm in San Francisco. Each year, they give the wrap to their clients as a gift in a promotion that involves the entire agency. For one thing, all the patterns come with names, and the names are varied and fun. Here's a sampling of the gift wrap names: Champagne, Tile, Geisha, Elephants, Monkeys, Octopi, Nightgown, Mints, Heat, Blossom, Flourish, Matrimony, Chill, Sputnik, Light, Cubist. Because naming the wraps is such a fun project, everyone in the studio participates in the naming process. As for the design itself, the inspiration comes from traditional Asian art combined with Modernism and a bit of contemporary Japanese graphics mixed in.

Anvil's promotional giftwrap started with 1,500 gift sets. Each year they increase the amount produced. They also partner with vendors so they can produce the gift wrap economically.

The project takes approximately four weeks from concept to completion. Ratliff explains, "The goal is always to produce the gift wrap in time to use as a holiday promotional gift for our clients. The short timeline also keeps our studio (labor) costs in check."

Alan Ratliff at Anvil describes the process: "We give the paper depth through use of varying color, line weight, scale, and opacity. The paper is designed to keep your eye moving so no matter how you wrap the gift the pattern will look beautiful from every angle. It's much like designing a scarf." To create the design is not simple and involves countless sketches, research, and lots of the aforementioned presentation meetings within the design firm. Ratliff notes, "Our biggest challenge was trying to select just six designs to include in our promotion. With everyone's enthusiasm and interest in the project, the staff produced more than fifty designs."

The gift wrap was a promotional idea that Alan had wanted to do for several years. "It not only promotes our creative capabilities but it provides a useful gift to the recipient. Because most of our work is in the high-tech industry, this was also a great opportunity for us to work on something completely different from our day-to-day projects."

Plans for the Future

So that's how it started. But it turns out that projects like this have a momentum all their own. Anvil received many compliments and won several awards. In fact, they got such great feedback from clients that they chose to test the waters of the wholesale market. In 2003 they sold the Neo Tokyo gift wrap line as flat sheets. For 2004 they decided to turn this into a business venture using national sales reps to sell the gift wrap in rolls and flat sheets. In an unabashed plug for the wrap, Ratliff adds, "Look for Anvil gift wrap at a design-conscious store near you or go to www.shopanvil.com for a list of stores and representatives."

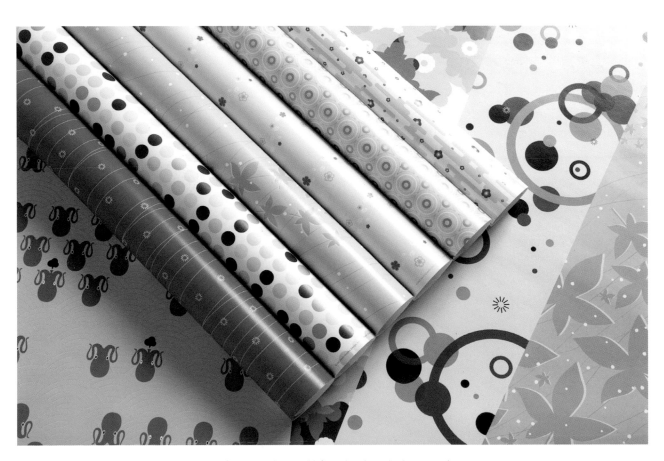

The gift wrap is a great reason to build relationships. Clients reveal personal information about who they wrapped a gift for and for which occasion. This window into their lives builds bonds, which strengthens client loyalty.

Design Firm   **Noon**

Client   **Noon**

Project   **Lunch-at-Noon Promotion**

Anyone Want to Go to Lunch?

"There once was a time when Monday's lunch was Sunday's leftovers or a cheap sandwich." —from Noon's website

This is no longer the case, thanks to a promotion by Noon, a San Francisco design firm with six designers and a philosophy based on "distinction, intelligence, and charisma." The group is close knit, and "agrees that we will always inform each other the day we begin to dread coming into work and we will always strive to do our best," notes Cinthia Wen, founder of the firm. This attitude extends even to the lunchtime hour, an hour particularly meaningful to an agency named Noon.

Cinthia explains. "We, as a group, do enjoy our time with each other and make the effort to spend lunch hour together daily. Thus, we created a 'game' where we each contributed to a collection of ingredients in a bowl. Then we each drew an ingredient from it weekly and brought a dish that we made with the ingredient the following Monday for a great big pot-luck lunch."

DESIGNS THAT STAND UP SPEAK OUT AND CANT BE IGNORED

A promotional mailing announcing a new website filled with recipes and food facts was created by Noon, a San Francisco design firm. The outside of the very personal-looking envelope is die-cut with a tiny place setting.

The aroma of dried rosemary greets the viewer when opening the package. The card merely states the Web address elegantly.

The announcements were sent mostly to friends and family as well as to a select group of clients and contacts. The mailing was simply to keep in touch with contacts, introduce a new project, and reinforce the studio's reputation of creative thinking.

The lunches at noon became so popular that it wasn't long before the team decided to create a website that would document all the recipes and photographs of the dishes. At first there was no intention in making the site public, but "the end product was surprisingly dear to us so we were compelled to share."

The Promotion That Almost Wasn't

And so, a promotion was born. The birth of the idea came from endless discussions among the designers about whether they should or should not announce the website upon completion. Eventually they agreed that if they could find a cost-effective and unique method for introducing the site, then they would. The criteria were that the promotional vehicle had to reflect the lunch-at-noon process itself as well as to have the look and feel of a special invitation.

Ahh, the Smell of Rosemary

The announcement itself is an intimate little card (5" x 3¼" [12.5 cm x 8 cm]) enclosed in a cream-colored envelope with die-cut icons of a knife, fork, and spoon on the front. When the recipient removes the card, they immediately are hit with the unmistakable smell of rosemary, as some dried sprigs are included with each card. The copy is nothing more than the website itself.

Two hundred and fifty of the promotions were created with a total teamwork effort. Hand-punching the die-cut envelopes got a bit painful, so everyone took turns. Drying the rosemary so that its oils didn't rub off onto the card was something that was taken into consideration and tested extensively.

For a promotion that almost wasn't, it ended up being amazingly successful. Soon after the mailing, the site was noted on the Yahoo! Hot List and Creative News. To Noon's surprise, the record hit on the site was 130,000 per month. Testament, perhaps, that when an idea is born out of true passion it always touches people in some way.

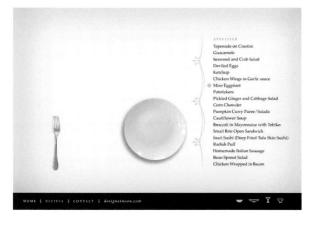

The website itself has dozens of recipes that were created by the designers at Noon. All recipes were tried and tested. In fact, each shot was taken moments before the designers dug in to eat.

Design Firm   **Red Canoe**
Client   **Cyr Studio**
Project   ***Axioms** Promotion*

Alignment

After writing *The Art of Promotion,* (Rockport Publishers, 2003) artist, author, and national lecturer Lisa L. Cyr was inspired to pursue a distinctive promotion of her own. "I was looking to attract the attention of the graphic arts industry from the major organizations, conferences, and universities to the trade media," recalls Cyr. With her eye for talent, she turned to Red Canoe as the firm of choice. "I love their sense of integrity, keen attention to detail, and most of all, their ability to communicate even to the most sophisticated audience," she adds. Cyr approached Deb Koch and Caroline Kavanagh, cofounders of Red Canoe, ("The Canoeists" as they like to be called), with a synergistic collaborative proposition.

After establishing a shared baseline measure for excellence under mutual philosophical and practical benchmarks, the two collaborators went to work and a promotional idea enthusiastically began to take shape. "Red Canoe believes that any promotion or brand extension must reveal an honest representation of the client's character," explains Koch. "In our research, we discovered that Cyr's writings and lectures consistently evolved around certain key words." For the *Axioms* promotion, the design team focused their attention on three in particular: Challenge, Pursuit, and Commitment. "These expressions are underlying constructs for any successful endeavor," comments Koch. "That is why we chose to use them as chapter headings, prominent themes in the promotion."

The French-folded front and back covers encase the hand-crafted, custom piece; all components were printed on an Epson 2200 printer. As a finishing touch, it is bound with screws and posts, securing actual rulers that accent the theme of measurement carried graphically throughout. The piece came mailed in a custom-fitted and labeled box along with a cover letter, business card with custom sleeve, and reply card. Order forms were also created to be sent as a follow-up on replies.

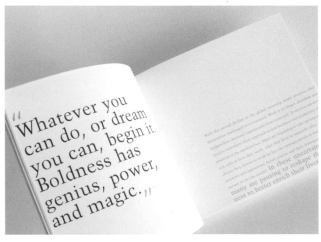

The book breaks down into three distinct chapters: Challenge, Pursuit, and Commitment. Challenge relates to not only the challenges that the industry faces but the challenges one makes venturing out with a unique voice and vision in a very competitive marketplace. Pursuit unfolds insight into how to stake a lasting claim in the often volatile business of visual communications. Lastly, commitment sheds light on how to put into action one's thoughts, goals, and dreams.

Structure

Because of the visual sophistication of the audience, the promotion had to far exceed the confines of a typical brochure. "When considering the approach, we were in pursuit of a visual vernacular that communicated on multiple levels with layered and interactive messages—interpretations that allowed a certain degree of audience definition," notes Koch. "Design, illustration, photography, and copy—these creative crafts always consider and reapproach perspective and context." The architecture for this promotion is structured with a keen attention to information design, from the title to the thought-provoking and almost definitional brain teasers that support each chapter heading. In addition, timeless, inspirational quotes are eloquently intermixed with real-world insight from seasoned professionals in a two-tiered typographical manner, an appropriate framework for Cyr's words of wisdom. The piece juxtaposes timeless, story-telling photography against vibrant, dynamic, and emotive illustrations. It was also important for the piece to display innovative production qualities, as the subtitle of *The Art of Promotion* is *Creating Distinction through Innovative Production Techniques*. The French-folded pages, tipped-in signature images, bindery, and custom identity elements each gave the recipient a sense of the kind of promotional vehicles that they were to experience in the book or at a lecture. All the details, both conceptual and production related, worked together to create an engaging and memorable experience.

Measure

Tackling the creation of a promotion entitled *Axioms* that is by definition "a proposition whose truth is so evident that no process of reasoning, of measuring, of demonstration can make it plainer—as the whole is greater than the parts" was surely not an easy course to take. But, in the end, it became a true measure of character. It not only talks the talk—it also walks the walk!

The theme of axioms—*self-evident, abstract truths—sets the tone and pacing of the book.*

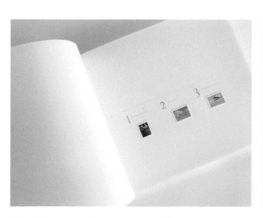

Each chapter opens with a salient quote from a significant industry professional juxtaposed against archival photographs enhanced with relevant schematic elements and accented by defining copy. The monochromatic, classic look of the photography is contrasted by the vividly colorful, more impressionistic art by leading contemporary illustrator Brian Cronin.

Design Firm   Angelini Design
Client   Angelini Design
Project   Corporate Brochure

The Importance of First Impressions

First impressions are a make it or break it proposition in today's overmarketed, oversaturated world. And it's especially important when it's a design firm making the first impression, since image is all they have. The first impression needs to be something that will make a potential client comfortable enough to want to spend tens of thousands of dollars on a design project.

Angelini Design knew they wanted something that could be delivered to potential clients to get them to accept the first telephone call. Something that would not only make a great first impression, but would clearly say that the design firm had a strong bias for high quality creative work and was passionate about the details.

Details, Details, Details

And the details of this particular piece are particularly noteworthy. Measuring just 5¾" x 7¼" (14.5 cm x 18.5 cm), the small, case-bound book has a black "shagreen" canvas cover and an engraved metallic badge carrying the Angelini logo on the front. The inside pages carry four-color printed images on 170 gr ivory Old Mill paper. The effect is elegant, rich, and tactile.

The brochure then gets packed in a black box and hand-delivered by courier directly to a database of marketing directors, top managers, PR managers of targeted companies, and advertising agencies. Each delivery is followed by the necessary telephone call. But by the time the phone rings, the potential client has a reason to remember Angelini Design.

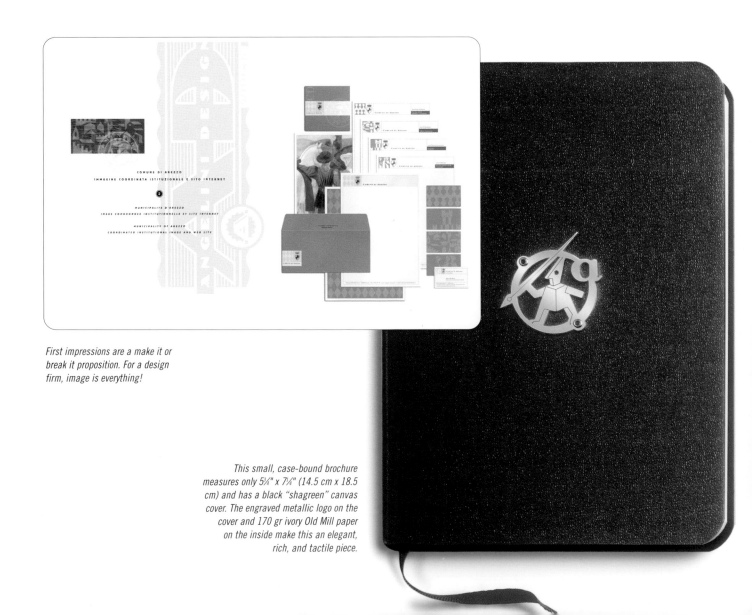

First impressions are a make it or break it proposition. For a design firm, image is everything!

This small, case-bound brochure measures only 5¾" x 7¼" (14.5 cm x 18.5 cm) and has a black "shagreen" canvas cover. The engraved metallic logo on the cover and 170 gr ivory Old Mill paper on the inside make this an elegant, rich, and tactile piece.

As Angelini designer Mariagrazia De Angelis notes, "Clients appreciate the strong personality of the brochure and the sense of prestige it communicates."

Mariagrazia goes on to note that the idea behind the brochure came from the *schetck book* (sketch book) that every Italian designer always keeps in his pocket and uses to spark creative inspiration throughout day. That's the reason why every page carries an unpublished *schetck* next to the published project. So not only does the client gain an appreciation for the finished design, but they also get to see the thinking that goes into an Angelini Design project firsthand.

Presentation Is Everything

And the showcased projects are many and varied—logos, brand identity, catalogs, company literature, brochures, packaging, trade shows, Internet graphic design, and point-of-purchase displays. There is packaging for Air Alitatia's snack box that actually makes airline food look good. Equally difficult, but equally well done, is packaging for a bra company logos and for Sony PlayStation and Peugeot. Samples of unusual design projects such as free-form-shaped mouse pads and cactus shaped salt and pepper shakers are also included.

What a beautiful way to package up such an eclectic mixture of projects!

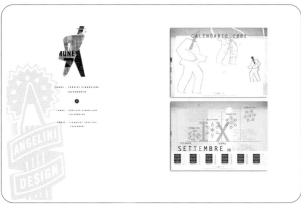

Angelini's projects are many and varied—logos, catalogs, brochures, packaging, and point-of-purchase displays are just a few types of design work showcased in their brochure.

Design Firm   **Emery Vincent Design**
Client   **Multiplex Lot 3**
Project   **Direct Mail Booklet**

Like Client, Like Promotion

A historic commercial property rich in texture and heritage deserves promotional material equally rich and textured, yes? That's certainly what Emery Vincent Design thought, even though most promotional materials in the commercial real estate category usually rely on high-color, glossy marketing materials.

Located at Wharf 8/9 on Sydney Harbour, Australia, the property is at once prestigious and unique, qualities that are echoed throughout the rich black-and-white photography and the sophisticated production. For example, the pages of the booklet were French-folded and bound together with silver interscrews, whereas the text on the cover was foil-stamped and debossed. The handmade slipcase also features foil stamping and debossed text.

The design strategy was to create a high-quality publication that was more like an art catalog than a sales brochure. A sense of elegance and sophistication is achieved through the use of black-and-white photography and is supported by abstract color imagery. This is reinforced by the restrained typography, which also references the buildings' historic past.

Most promotional materials for commercial real estate are glossy four-color pieces. Emery Vincent Design took a unique and tactile approach to highlight a property that is itself unique and tactile.

A sense of elegance and sophistication is achieved through the use of black-and-white photography and the restrained typography, which also references the buildings' historic past.

Sending It Out

The brochure was mainly distributed by direct mail to top 500 Australian companies, with a particular emphasis on entrepreneurs with a potential interest in securing a one-off location on Sydney Harbour. It was thought that these people would most likely appreciate the uniqueness of the property itself: it is the last intact complex of its type in the world and the best example of early 1900s Sydney port infrastructure.

The brochure needed to promote the opportunity to buy a unique slice of historic real estate right on Sydney Harbour—a never-to-be repeated offer. But there were certainly barriers to be overcome. For example, communicating the exact location and its future potential was a challenge, given that the rejuvenation of the area was not yet complete and the location did not have a strong identity. Also, the brochure was effectively asking someone to buy in an up-and-coming location (for which they would normally expect a discount) but at a premium price.

In this instance, ego was an important button to press. The idea was that there would be very few individuals who could afford such an exquisite yet underdeveloped location. And the design, with all its rich details, spoke to that ego.

What's in a Name?

The name Lot 3 was chosen because the development is located on Lot 3 and the property is unique enough not to require a clever metaphorical. It also leverages the Sotheby's connection (offered through Sotheby's International Realty), a company that deals in historic rarities for wealthy individuals. The end result is a brochure that feels rich and rare and one of a kind.

The design strategy was to create a high-quality publication that was more like an art catalog than a sales brochure.

Design Firm   Sandstrom Design
Client   Portland Center Stage
Project   Identity System and Promotional Materials

Designers to the Rescue

Portland Center Stage is the largest live theater production company in Portland, Oregon, yet it was plagued by static attendance and growing financial problems as it entered its fifteenth season. So when the theater company hired a new artistic director, Chris Coleman, it was clear he had to do *something*. And with the help of Sandstrom Design, they did something remarkable.

The To-Do List

The goals were challenging: first, to improve the quality and diversity of the performances, and second, to build a national reputation. Although Portland Center Stage took responsibility for the first goal, Sandstrom Design quickly attacked the second. They began to redesign the identity system, as well as all promotional materials for Portland Center Stage. The identity system included a new logo and stationery, and general guidelines for their usage on mailers, print ads, banners, and apparel. The promotional materials included posters, flyers, mailers, print ads, playbills, and many other pieces. The lead piece was a small 56-page flyer that outlines the play schedule for the 2003–2004 year. It was mailed to all previous subscribers and potential customers on a targeted mailing list, handed out at every performance, and distributed as a rack brochure in a variety of venues around town.

A poster series with a unified graphic look helped the Portland Center Stage achieve its goal of national recognition. Powerful graphics, bright colors, and evocative images were used to showcase each performance.

Flyers to promote future events were bundled up like newspapers and given out at performances.

Performing arts communities are fairly small, often less than 4 percent of a city's total population. The upside to that statistic is that it's fairly easy to identify that target, which makes it efficient to market to them. They are educated, urban dwellers who periodically attend the ballet, opera, and symphony. They range in age from 25 to 65 and tend to sample the arts first and then subscribe later. Because the performing arts are dependent upon donors to stay afloat, many of them are charitable givers and convert to donors after becoming subscribers.

Breaking Away from the Competition

The concept used for the flyer stressed the fact that this is live theater. This distanced Portland Center Stage from television and movies as an entertainment option. Live theater is more compelling, tends to involve the audience more intimately, and often allows them to interact with the performers and positively affect the quality of the play.

The copy states: "The experience, at its core, is a provocative relationship. The actors take the stage and offer themselves up to the audience. They tell a story, evoke an image, and conjure an emotion. The audience reacts, and from this energy emerges a performance that can never again be replicated. You are cordially invited to shape the following performances . . ."

This concept came directly from an interview with the artistic director. Coleman talked passionately about live theater as a total sensory feedback experience. His love of his work and his level of dedication inspired the designers to bring his insight to the attention of the subscriber base.

Money is always an issue with performing arts groups, and that's when reality hit the production process. Sandstrom's recommendation was significantly above Portland Center Stage's budget, and there needed to be a reduction in colors, size, and pages to come closer to it. The end result was close approximation of the original design, and other elements of the marketing program were eliminated to cover the costs.

Building Awareness

To achieve the goal of national recognition, Sandstrom recommended that the poster series be consistent through the year. A concept was created that was based upon rock band poster art. Powerful graphics, bright colors, and evocative images were used to showcase each performance. Larry Jost was hired to illustrate each poster, and each poster is more powerful than the one before. You might say that the posters come to life, just like the theatrical presentations.

Larry Jost illustrated each poster in the style of rock band poster art, and each poster is more powerful than the one before.

The lead piece was a small 56-page flyer that outlines the play schedule for the 2003–2004 year. The concept revolves around the fact that this is live theater, and the copy "cordially invites the audience to shape the following performances."

Design Firm   Viva Dolan Communications & Design Inc.

Client   ArjoWiggins Fine Papers

Project   Curious Direct Mailer

How do you make someone curious?

a) Give them something to open that's wrapped up like a giant stick of gum.

b) Prominently feature a bald guy and a penguin.

c) Show four unique kinds of paper.

d) All of the above.

Yes, all of the above. Well, it certainly made *us* curious.

So, what is this project that invokes such curiosity? It is a direct mail piece. It's sized to fit in a standard DL envelope. It's printed on a representative cross-section of the Curious Collection of papers. And it was produced in 12 languages for 20 markets worldwide with the target audience being the European design and advertising community.

It's hard to resist opening something wrapped up like a giant stick of gum— silver foil with pinking-sheared edges.

Inside are four inserts with engaging visuals. The only copy is the word new *printed in seven different languages.*

The Beginnings

The project started when ArjoWiggins Fine Papers, design firm Viva Dolan's Anglo-French client, consolidated several legacy brands under one umbrella to create the Curious Paper Collection. This consolidation strategy was subsequently adopted worldwide, with Viva Dolan acting as the lead branding/design firm. The Canada-based design firm provided creative direction, graphic design, writing/editorial, and intensive production management for a program of swatchbooks, brochures, and packaging. The program was aimed at twenty markets in twelve different languages, using seven printers in four countries. The aim was to make the Curious Paper Collection the most effective, smart, visually striking, strategically branded, beautifully produced project imaginable.

When ArjoWiggins Fine Papers asked Viva Dolan to help them with the launch, they had been a client since 1991, so the design firm had a good understanding of what was needed. They produced a boxed set of introductory swatchbooks, which visually spoke to the unique characteristics of each paper, as well as a print advertising campaign and a website using the same design strategy.

Stop Teasing

So where does this small promotional piece fit in—a piece meant to be a teaser, designed merely to arouse curiosity in the Curious brand? It's a piece that uses snippets of the imagery (without giving too much away) from the Curious Collection swatchbooks due for release later in the year.

The piece is a series of five simple samples of the paper with minimal copy and the curious illustrations on them. Each piece was designed, printed, and photographed according to a tight pencil sketch. The photographer and illustrators had access to the sketch and produced precise images that fit into the layout. The end result is a whimsical promotion cool enough to have been featured in British *D&AD* and *AIGA*.

Now for Something Trivial

And as for that bald guy: He's a French-Canadian named Jean-Luis; he was the model for a Metallics hair dye box that Viva Dolan designed. They dyed his hair gray for the shot, and when he attempted to dye it back to his natural color, it turned blue. He then shaved his head in frustration.

Just in case you were curious.

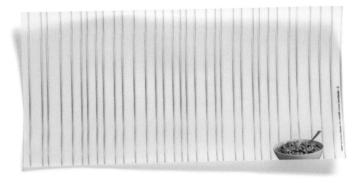

The inserts are printed on a variety of papers: "Translucents patterned with diamonds and snake scales. Particles that shimmer and vanish with body heat. And a textured sheet that ripples and droops like damp floppy fabric."

At some point, you become an adult and things start coming together. You make choices and realize they are your choices and no one else's. Perhaps you do the proverbial "settling down" or perhaps you travel the world. You've found a career calling that suits you or you hop around trying new ones. Responsibility is not the heavy word with a capital R that it once was. Sure, you have responsibilities, but in the end, that's just day-to-day life. You make choices about yourself, your family, your future, and you live with them. And so most of the people in this age group have at least a semblance of having life figured out. And it's great.

Market to the adult age group, and you're casting a wide net. This group is not tied together by age as much as teens are. Still, there are some commonalities. People in this age group are making wise choices, and they are making them more and more intuitively. They have a variety of interests but are not so set in their ways that they won't try new things.

So when a tiny arts center in the United Kingdom wants to get its name in front of as many people in this age group as possible, what do they do? They come up with an innovative promotional idea, and then run with it.

They blanket the Great North Run—Britain's biggest running event—with signs that tap into the psyche of this demographic. Playing off the B in the name, the Baltic Contemporary Arts Centre sponsors an entire campaign that revolves around the way people of this age feel. *B.Great. B.Determined. B.Lucky. B.Excited. B.Limber. B.Ready.*

Design Firm **Blue River Design**
Client **Baltic**
Project **Baltic Centre B.Great**

When the Baltic Contemporary Arts Centre wanted to appeal to the 27- to 45-year-old target, they blanketed one of Britain's largest race events with banners that spoke directly to the psyche of the audience.

The signs evoked the curiosity of many spectators, who asked about the Baltic Center or even volunteered to hold some of the signs.

This well-known half marathon was identified as a suitable vehicle to use to take the Baltic brand outside of its usual environment and engage and interact with an audience directly at street level. The half marathon's audience and emotion levels matched those of the Baltic Contemporary Arts Centre. The race also offered huge audience figures with its 47,000 runners plus the potential to capitalize on the guaranteed national and regional media coverage. The starting point of the race was in close proximity to the Arts Centre, which added an extra element of fusion on the day of the race.

Baltic was able to tap directly into the carnival-style feel at street level, bonding with both runners and spectators. The team of banner holders was frequently questioned about the banners as well as the activities, exhibitions, and projects at Baltic. Some of the public spectators even offered to hold the banners. The banners provided an approachable, friendly face for Baltic. Baltic was, without a doubt, able to engage directly with its target audience and help them develop a strong emotional bond with the Baltic brand.

A great way to B.Great.

The promotion not only got the attention of more than 47,000 runners and spectators, but there was extensive media coverage, which often included shots of the simple, yet powerful signs.

What makes a promotion successful? Roll the dice and find out . . .

Everything a Client Could Ask For

From a "drinking game cube" to a draft beer tap handle that includes the svelte curves of a woman on the handle, Hornall Anderson Design Works, a design firm in Seattle, created the promotional materials that would successfully brand Widmer Brothers' Blonde Ale. The agency designed everything from the beer's six-pack carrier, bottles, poster, metal sign, beer tap handle, T-shirt, and fact sheet to the drinking game cube.

Not only do the promotional collateral pieces incorporate the look and feel of the brand, but they do so in a creative way. For example, the drinking game cube is a memorable and whimsical way to promote the brand because it actually serves a purpose. Customers can keep the item, instead of receiving just another flyer or card advertising the brand that begs to be thrown away. The blonde character on the tap handle becomes very recognizable when lined up with numerous other tap handles in a bar or pub. It speaks for the brand not only through its name, but also through its visual impact.

The drinking game cube is a fun and interactive way to keep the Blonde Ale name in front of drinkers. Roll the dice . . . then propose a toast, add a new rule, or ask a buddy to drink.

Speaking Out to a Small Crowd

The target audience for this beer is relatively narrow—males, ages 21 to 28, and consumers of microbrew beers. So, you have a beer named Blonde Ale, and you have males who are just past the drinking age and . . . well, suffice it to say that using images of svelte blonde women and encouraging the target to play a drinking game was inordinately successful.

Brand Image Is Key

But the successful Blonde Ale brand had an interesting history. It proves the point that success or failure of a beer is never based on taste alone; it is the resulting brand image that surrounds any given flavor that makes it successful in the marketplace. This particular flavor of beer was originally launched by Widmer under the name Sweet Betty, and a brand character was created around a 1940s-era woman. When launched, however, sales of the beer were notably lackluster. It was determined that not only did the character not appeal as much to the target audience, but the name Sweet Betty left consumers assuming it was a sweet-tasting beer as well. Sweet Betty, had to go. Christina Arbini, media relations manager at Hornall Anderson, explains, "To find a stronger appeal in the marketplace, we renamed the beer 'Blonde Ale,' and reintroduced the character as a svelte, hip, sophisticated woman. This new brand appealed to both male and female consumers."

A Satisfied Customer

The project started out as a packaging and collateral request only. As the design project developed, the client felt that the concept and execution were so strong that the project extended itself to a tacker sign, table tent, drinking cube, and a tap handle. The client thought that Hornall Anderson Design Works created the perfect package solution that represented not only the personality of the Widmer Brothers brand of products but also dramatically improved the current sales records for the Blonde Ale line. After all, beer sales speak for themselves.

The promotional materials were designed for Widmer Brothers Blonde Ale after it was determined that the original flavor name— Sweet Betty—simply did not resonate with the target audience.

The new character was the perfect match for their target market, 21- to 28-year-old males.

The Machine Age. An era when machines enhanced living and mass production, and glorified streamlining. According to Michael Hodgson of Ph.D in Los Angeles, California, the Machine Age "was the most important iconoclastic revolutionary movement of the last century."

Eight Is Enough

And so a trio of posters, all titled "eight," celebrate the look of graphic design in the Machine Age. The reason for their being is apt enough—to announce the acquisition of a new eight-color Heidelberg Press at printer Primary Color. As copy from the posters proudly proclaims, "Primary Color brings an eight-color machine of opus proportions to the forefront of its own operation. Surrounded by specialists with keen eyes and unsurpassed attention to details. Light speed ahead."

The Machine Age period of design occurred from the middle 1920s through World War II, an era that swung between euphoria and sobriety. Machine Age graphics were usually black-and-white, with the odd spot of color. Ph.D wanted the posters to have the look of their original counterparts, but be produced in lavish, luxurious ways. According to Hodgson, "Most printers overplay their hand . . . we wanted people to see these posters, touch them, and ask 'How the hell did they do that?'"

The idea behind this set of three bold posters from Ph.D was to highlight the eight-color press capabilities of printer Primary Color.

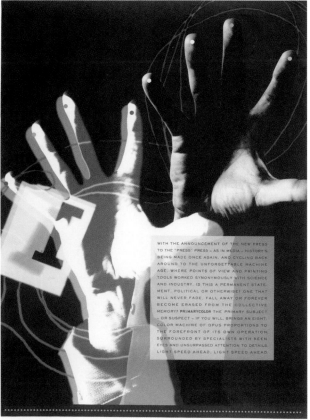

The look for all of the posters was based on Machine Age graphic design.

A Gala Event

The series of three 24" x 36" (61 cm x 91.4 cm) posters was distributed at a gala event. At the same time the press was being put in place at Primary Color, Ph.D was busily designing a new identity for the printer. An open house was held to announce the new identity, and at the event posters were rolled and presented to clients and vendors along with goodie bags. Also, large-format versions of the posters were made to grace the walls at the open house.

Ron Slenzack photographed two of the posters. For the one titled "eight" (whoops, they're all titled "eight") the design firm obtained the rights to use a Tennessee Valley Authority photograph, which "playfully suggests the importance" of the new press. The figures along the disappearing sight line were retouched over the original photo. Also of note is that each poster was printed on a different paper type, ranging from an 80# gloss cover to a 50# smooth text to a 92# metallic anodized cover. A range of spot colors, Pantone Matching System colors, varnishes, and foils were also used, albeit sparingly to demonstrate the printer's range.

History Repeats Itself

"History is being made once again cycling back around to the unforgettable Machine Age. Where points of view and printing tools worked synonymously with science and industry." So states another blurb of copy from the posters, with the posters themselves being testament to that statement.

From start to finish, the project took three months to complete. Printing on that new eight-color press, however, was a breeze. After all, light speed ahead.

Ph.D likes to produce work that has "a cleverness to it and perhaps a sense of wit," remarks Michael Hodgson, who helped art direct the piece along with Clive Piercy and Heather Caughey.

Design Firm   Ph.D
Client   Roxy
Project   Roxy Vibe Promotion

A photo shoot that lasts four days and is held on the Big Island of Hawaii. Ahhh, life is good!

Calling All Girls

The shoot was for a promotional piece for Roxy, the junior girls' line of Quicksilver's apparel and a leading brand for active girls. It's designed for the "junior customer with progressive style who embraces all elements of life," explains Michael Hodgson, of Ph.D, Quicksilver's design firm. The Roxy girl is "involved in beach sports and snow sports and demands a girly fit and functional wear." The line is designed by Dana Dartez, who designs clothes ranging from basic surfwear for sport and style to vintage-inspired, forward-looking sportswear. The brand was launched in 1991 with a line of swimwear, but quickly expanded to include surf clothing, snow wear, denim, footwear, accessories, fragrances, and skin care. Tying all the product lines together is a soulful, spiritual vibe that defines the more ethereal nature of the brand Roxy.

Roxy sells a complete line of products for young, active girls in the United States, Europe, and Australia.

A Soulful, Spiritual, Surfing Feeling

And so that youthful, soulful, spiritual, surfing feeling—part girly, part vintage, progressive, embracing-life feeling is what California-based Ph.D wanted to capture in a promotional piece to be given out at trade shows. The idea they created is a 30-page, 5½" x 8½" (14 cm x 21.6 cm) booklet that has gorgeous four-color photography interspersed with vellum sheets. On the vellum sheets are lovely brush illustrations by Ann Field. The photographs show through the vellum, and they interact with the illustrations to add an element of whimsy and surprise. For example, an illustration of a surfer is deep blue with ominous shadows behind it. When you turn the page, you realize the photography below the vellum is an underwater shot of two surfer girls kicking on top of the water.

The idea for the illustrated vellum sheets grew out of the fact that Roxy's new branding image involves a sense of transparency—there's a sense of always seeing through to the next level. This comes across in the vellum, the images of water and sky, and the illustrations, which are done in watercolor to further enhance the idea of transparency.

Hard-working Models

The catalog is also notable for the fact that the Roxy models are all excellent amateur or professional surfers. Megan Abubo, for example, is part of the World Championship Tour of surfers. And Lisa Anderson is a four-time world champion and the first woman to be inducted in the Hall of Fame of Surfing. In fact, Lisa is often credited with changing the image and perception of the sport of women's surfing, according to Roxy's website. She "became a role model for young women and girls everywhere, proving that a girl can rip and still possess femininity."

The entire piece took just three weeks to create from start to finish. The short time frame created a frenzied pace, a fact the designers lamented.

But then, don't feel sorry for them. After all, there was that photo shoot in Hawaii.

The promotional piece was designed with vellum inserts, which add a layer of transparency and interact with the photographs in surprising ways. This piece was created to be given away at trade shows.

All Roxy models are amateur and professional surfers. Lisa, for example, is a four-time world champion.

Salon. A word that reached its height of popularity around the turn of the century—the long-ago turn of the century in 1900, that is. A salon was a place where prominent people from the worlds of literature, art, music, and politics met on a regular basis.

A Thoroughly Modern Salon

More than a hundred years later, we now have, appropriately enough, a "Digital Salon." The intent is still the same as the salon days of yore, but with a thoroughly modern twist. In this case, Salon Digital opens its doors once a month at the Cross Media Lab of the Academy of Art and Design in Offenbach, Germany. Two prominent academics, Rotraut Pape and Bernd Kracke, invite between 100 and 150 well-known artists, producers, and designers for a *jour fixe* with professors as well as students. The invited guests show actual film, video, or other media projects and then discuss their insights with the audience. Different topics are presented, such as streaming projects of the Berlin music scene and independent media projects in international political context.

Such an event needs to be promoted on a regular basis to inform and attract the people most likely to attend—the students, the people from other academies and universities, and, of course, all persons generally interested in culture. Posters are the perfect promotional vehicle to grace the halls of academia where the target audience hangs out.

A series of posters designed to promote Salon Digital, a monthly gathering of prominent people from the arts and academia who gather together to discuss, in this case, streaming media.

Two hundred posters are produced for each run. Although they are created using only simple lines, the posters have a rich quality due to the fanciful type and illustration and the black and gold color scheme.

Squiggly and Baroque

The design firm Hesse, a 16-year-old institution in the German design scene, was called in. They wanted to pick up on some design conventions that echoed the feeling of the turn of the twentieth century. Klaus Hesse, a principal of the firm and a designer, teacher, illustrator, and typographer, has a love of type that extends back to his student days at the Bergische Universität Wuppertal. Klaus says that what he loves most about design is "the idea and the second view." Thus, it was immediately apparent to him that the style of the type and illustration should be "a little squiggled and baroque" to echo the original time period of the salon. And because the lecture series is known as Salon Digital, the type and illustration are done with one tool that is both artistic and digital: Freehand.

The posters are monochromatic (the first three were in gold and the fourth in black). Although they are done in lines only, they have a richness all their own. The design is flexible enough to accommodate different needs yet retain its design integrity. At the beginning of a new series with new guest speakers the colors might shift, along with a variation in the style of illustration. Still done with Freehand, still squiggly, but a variety of looks can be created within those parameters.

The response has been overwhelming. Visitors of the Salon Digital not only had a great salon experience, but they took the posters home afterward. Out of 200 that had been produced, not one was left at the venue.

The "squiggly and baroque" style of illustration was done using the designer's favorite tool, Freehand.

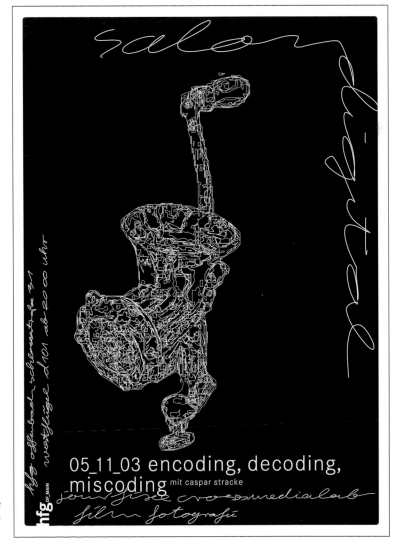

Klaus Hesse, principal of the design firm and also typographer and illustrator of the series, has a love of type that is very apparent in his work.

Design Firm **Giorgio Davanzo Design**
Client **Giorgio Davanzo Design**
Project **The Hidden Agenda of Dreams Book**

Look through the exquisite bound book with the intriguing title *The Hidden Agenda of Dreams*. You will see that dreams containing trains often represent opportunities in life, dreams containing clowns often represent "a deep and heavily camouflaged sadness or dissatisfaction," and dreams containing boats suggest a subconscious thinking of problems in romantic relationships. In analyzing these dreams and their meanings, we might also wonder: what does a dream, dreamt by Giorgio Danvanzo, about a handbook of dreams suggest? As it turns out, it suggests a startlingly effective self-promotional piece, in the form of a very real 4¾" by 6⅜" (12 cm x 16.2 cm) booklet. A booklet whose sole purpose seems to be to analyze dreams.

Enticing the Reader

The Hidden Agenda of Dreams, at first glance, looks like a book of the sort you might find in an antique bookstore run by an enchantress. It is simple and elegant, a mere 26 pages long, mostly black and white, with a gold title and no author. However, upon further inspection, one can see that not only is it a book, but it is a tool with a dual purpose. For the receiver, it is a tool for analyzing dreams. For its creator, Giorgio Davanzo Design, it is for promoting his design company in the simplest, most effective way—promoting yourself by not promoting. Instead of promoting with the usual tools of loud graphics and attention-grabbing colors, he used a "compelling subject matter, refined art direction, and high production values." The compelling subject matter took twelve images that routinely appear in dreams and analyzed their deeper meaning in a few sentences.

The Hidden Agenda of Dreams *is a self-promotion piece for Giorgio Davanzo Design that is cleverly disguised as a beautiful little book that analyzes dreams and their meanings.*

A Promotion That's Like a Dream

This simplicity and beauty was able to "seduce even the most promotion-resistant" audience, which in this case consisted of 500 existing and prospective clients who received the handbook in a cream-colored, cloth shipping bag. Giorgio Davanzo Design wanted to show clients what the design firm could do in an "unusual and memorable way." At the same time, there was also awareness that these clients were bombarded every day with thousands of advertisements and designs in the form of everything from pop-ups to logos on sweatshirts. Knowing that by using the same tactics, it would be too easy to get lost in the chaos of promotions, Giorgio decided that there was no need to shout when he could convey his message more powerfully in a whisper. As he states, the beauty of the book is that "it's so gutsy in its subtlety."

However, the greatest irony is the similarity in the triangle of dreams, the handbook, and promotions. The prologue of the handbook ends with "In your lifetime, you will have over 150,000 dreams. What are they trying to tell you?" A promotion is just like a dream. You will see thousands. What are they trying to tell you? Which ones will you remember? Which of them will come back time and time again to haunt you, in ways that make you unlikely to forget?

The refined art direction and high production value came in the form of elegant typeface, and beautiful photography—duotones and black-and-white photos that were attained by painstakingly searching through the Library of Congress website.

What will you dream of tonight?

"Dream No. 11. Boat. Traveling on water is common when we are dreaming about romantic relationships or interpersonal conflicts. Water is associated with deep emotional feelings. Sailing is a metaphor for how you feel currently about your life, your degree of control, and your level of satisfaction. Are you at the helm?"

The idea literally came to Giorgio in a dream. But after designing the piece, he "realized in horror that all the dreams were in Italian. He needed the help of a writer. But not just any writer. He wanted Gretchen Lauber, the über-talented copywriter, jetsetter, renowned art collector, and Pinot Noir expert."

Design Firm   **Dynamo Art & Design**

Client   **V Pliant**

Project   **Identity/Promotion Materials**

V Pliant is a company that sells clothing and bags that have an interesting, edgy combination of vintage textures and materials. So it only makes sense that the promotional materials for such a company would also have an interesting, edgy combination of vintage textures and materials. From vellum to old postcards to grommets to metallic thread to rubber stamping on variable cloth, the promotional materials are a recycling dream come true. If it works, use it.

Clothing That's Recycled and Reconstructed . . .

A small, independent company producing what they call "reconstructed clothing," V Pliant sells one-of-a-kind items made from vintage, unusual, reclaimed materials. The identity system likewise incorporates industrial, old, and modern elements and handcrafting techniques. The company information, for example, is rubber stamped onto the back of the business card and hangtag, which is layered with paper ephemera using grommets. The logo is also stamped onto various cloth squares to create sew-in labels, and the letterhead is printed onto vellum and backed with varying pieces of paper ephemera.

. . . And an Identity That's the Same

Not only does the creative approach mesh with that of V Pliant, but also it's a philosophy that Dynamo Art & Design embraces with all clients. Nina Wishnok, principal of the Boston-based agency, has four guiding principals for great design: 1) Don't self-edit too much early on in the process because you never know where something's going to lead; 2) Look anywhere and everywhere for inspiration; 3) Leave plenty of room for (and welcome!) happy accidents; and 4) Stay flexible.

It took five months from the initial meeting to completion of the project, which included hangtags, sew-in labels, business cards, and letterhead. The pieces are used for products, shows, resellers, direct-sale customers, and correspondence.

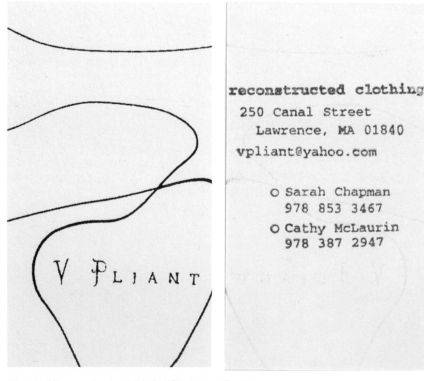

The look of the promotional materials for V Pliant takes off on the definition of the word "pliant," which calls to mind lines and movement, which led to the abstract line work of the logo, a mark that suggests metal wire or thread.

The sew-in labels for the clothing were made from various scraps of leftover cloth that were then rubber stamped.

An Idea Is Born

The birth of the idea came through intellectual discussions at the first meeting. The client and design firm spoke the same language, and thus were able to discuss ideas together with ease. Ideas that otherwise might scare all but the most visually literate client—abstract design concepts like appropriation and recontextualization, and visual ideas such as repetition, irregularity, texture, layering, asymmetry, and juxtaposition. As a result of such a discussion, Nina began thinking about using materials that brought a sense of past life, materials that were previously used or evocative in some way—all characteristics of the materials and treatments V Pliant uses for their clothing.

The production challenges were, for the most part, due to budget. But out of such restrictions, resourcefulness is born. The client was hesitant to spend too much money on printing sew-in labels for the garments and bags. So Wishnok suggested using rubber stamps, which saved on printing costs and also suited the industrial, funky, V Pliant aesthetic. This brought flexibility and variability to the materials, which turned out to be one of the most interesting aspects of the system.

The response to the materials has been very positive. The client loves it because it's flexible and variable but still coherent. Vendors and customers say it really fits the V Pliant personality and products.

The hangtags were made using old postcards together with vellum, grommets, metallic thread, and rubber stamping.

The letterhead was created by rubber stamping the logo on vellum, then folding it into various found materials such as wrapping paper and magazine pages.

The brief from the client was simple. Wales Arts International didn't have much money, but wanted to "create an interesting identity that would inspire." The identity needed to promote the council as an organization that cares about the image of contemporary Wales and is interested in the benefits that international collaboration can bring. And the client had one mandate: "We like strong, bold, confident colors."

Small Budget, Big Look

So Elfen, a design firm in Wales, started the project with gusto. Most of their clients have small budgets, so they were no strangers to limited funds.

The new identity for Wales Arts International needed to include letterheads, compliment slips, business cards, folders, and moving announcements. The target audience is the international arts scene, which includes artists and arts organizations in Wales.

Wales Arts International is a partnership between the Arts Council of Wales and British Council of Wales that works to promote knowledge about contemporary culture from Wales. Both organizations encourage international exchange and collaboration and help build a dynamic international context for the local arts. Established in 1997, the organization undertakes project work that promotes and develops contemporary art form practice and supports individual artists and arts organizations to explore international partnerships.

The goal of re-branding Wales Arts International was to portray an organization that cares about the image of contemporary Wales and is interested in the benefits that international collaboration can bring.

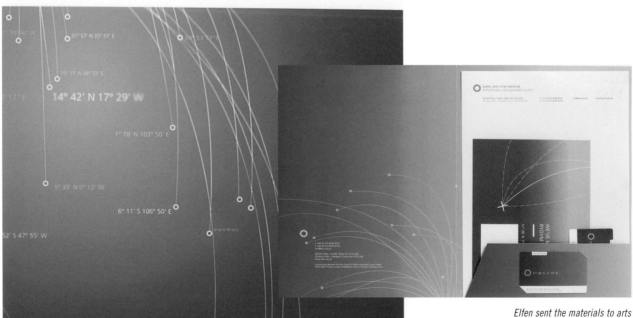

Elfen sent the materials to arts organizations all over the world. They also sent it to funding bodies and individual artists in Wales and abroad.

Marking a Location

So the birth of the idea occurred from the original client brief—it contained a list of all the British embassies around the world with which Wales Arts International is connected. The identity uses a strikingly simple graphic of location markers, showing Wales Arts International's position geographically and connecting it graphically to the points where the British embassies are. This created an underlying theme for Elfen's work for the client, and each time they approach a new project, the theme gave inspiration to create something new within the same idea. To generate interest in and knowledge of the organization, Elfen established a design and logo that would withstand time, was effective, and was understood internationally.

Elfen also devised a creative production process for printing materials that looked very high-end on a limited budget. The printwork uses cyan, magenta, yellow and black (CMYK) inks but is set up as specials so that they can create three-color print using, say, the yellow, magenta, and black or any other three color combinations. This process keeps the customer print cost low, as most presses are set up for CMYK, and Elfen only ends up using three plates. Or if the job requires full-color image printing, the full CMYK achieves the same result for the logo. The identity has four versions of the logo in different colors. Color calibration had to be noted for consistency from project to project, as all the colors depended on two of the CMYK range and were printed at a high density.

The end result? Bold, strong, confident colors, just like the client ordered.

Guto Evans explains Elfen's philosophy: "We are driven by ideas, even if we are just working on a letterhead! The best projects always have ideas behind them; if people read into them, they decide for themselves what that may be. But if anyone asks, 'So how did you come to this design?' we always have an answer."

The Wales Arts International promotional materials were received with much interest. The design style met positive comments from existing and potential clients and partners.

Design Firm   **Evolve Design**
Client   **Evolve**
Project   **Self-Promotional Book**

An eight-month labor of love that leads to an incredible return on investment. That's the long and short of *Sixty-four Printed Leaves*, a lovely 128-page, case-bound, self-promotional book that highlights the portfolio of London-based design firm Evolve.

The book is "used to accompany tender documents, or in presentations where supporting credentials are required," explains designer Jonathon Hawkes. Its uncoated plain brown cover is embossed with an intricate leaf pattern. Inside, the smooth white pages carry glossy, colorful examples of Evolve's work.

A Soft Sell

Evolve is a small partnership of designers with no sales team and no business developers. They are often too immersed in design work to develop new contacts and search for the next big project, and as a result they have quiet periods. *Sixty-four Printed Leaves* was produced to do the soft sell on the design firm's behalf.

This little pocket book is deliberately understated, reflecting the size and philosophy of Evolve. It is small and accessible, yet substantial. As Hawkes notes, "I'm always suspicious of companies that shout about themselves. If a product is good, it should speak for itself. This book lets our work do the talking."

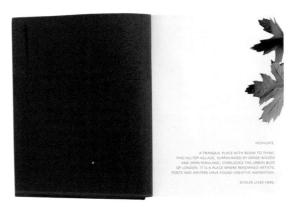

The book sets the stage for an environmentally focused design firm that is housed in the woods. "Highgate. A tranquil place with room to think. This Hilltop village surrounded by dense woods and open parkland overlooks the urban buzz of London. Evolve lives here."

Sixty-four Printed Leaves *is a subtle play on words—it's the technical description of the 128-page book, but also refers to the environment that Evolve loves so much.*

The remaining 50 pages showcase Evolve's work, which includes identity systems, stationery, brochures, sales promotions, and magazine advertisements.

Inspiration Was Right Outside the Window

The genesis of the idea stemmed from the desire to separate Evolve from dozens of similar-sized competitors by projecting a unique and memorable image. Evolve operates from a large treetop studio, in the beautiful leafy village of Highgate, North London. This alone helps paint a mental picture. Combined with the fact that a large proportion of the work the firm produces is environmental literature, it made sense to use the natural surroundings as a selling point. The embossed structure on the cover is taken from one of the branches that presses up against the studio windows.

Although Hawkes readily admits he's no copywriter, the words are as equally well crafted as the design. He insists, "It's just sheer luck. I guess all those late nights writing design proposals have rubbed off."

Attention to Detail

The production process speaks to the design firm's attention to detail. Once the color had dried, the gloss varnish and metallic silver were run through the press in a second pass to maximize their shine. The metallic silver text adds brightness throughout the book and works equally well on both white pages and dark photos. The only real problem encountered was with the cover emboss, which started out as much deeper. Unfortunately, air bubbles developed at the gluing stage, so the emboss die was altered. This gave a more subtle result.

Also of note is that committing to print, rather than merely updating an ever-changing website, means Evolve is now treated with more maturity. Their projects are becoming more substantial. The success of their book speaks to the power of print, in an age where electronic communication is the norm.

Although the immediate cost was sizable (GBP £8,000 to print 1,000 copies), the return on investment was immediate and gratifying. The first commission it helped generate was worth GBP £60,000. More importantly, it's bringing in the right kind of work—greener projects. Since the promotion has been put in place, Evolve has been commissioned to produce an environmental training program, a series of documents on historic architecture, and an environmental report for the Ford Motor Company.

The first few pages speak of the design firm and the people who work there. The text describes Donna: "Training in the discipline of traditional copyfitting has made her the creative yet artisanal typographer she is today." And Jonathan, for whom "endless hours are spent capturing the proverbial thousand words in a single frame."

The promotion has generated more of the kinds of projects that Evolve loves the most—environmental ones. They already had good experience in the field, which deserved to be showcased. Here are some spreads from a book the design firm did for the Henry Ford European Conservation Awards.

Design Firm **Dinnick + Howells**

Client **The Water Drop**

Project **Graphic and Retail Design Program**

Water. Needed by all, yet largely taken for granted.

A Store That Sells Water

For example, when asked what 75 percent of our brain is made of, water does not usually come to mind. We complain when it rains and complain about the prices of bottled water. Even the color of water is, well, invisible. Therefore, Dinnick + Howells had a challenging task in front of them when they took on the retail client The Water Drop. This is because The Water Drop isn't any store; it's a store dedicated to selling only water. How could Dinnick + Howell create a design out of the element that is so largely ignored and can barely be seen?

Enter into the store called The Water Drop. You will feel like you are entering a place that is part museum, part artsy boutique.

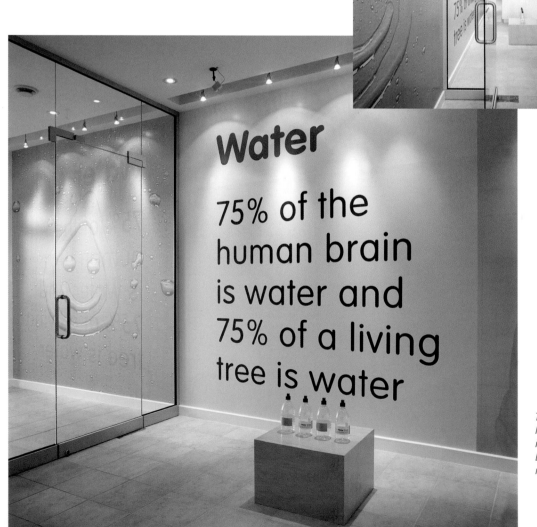

The strategy was to create a visual language that celebrated water—its importance to human health, its beauty, and its relationship to the natural world.

The Message Is in the Mascots

What they came up with was the idea of water mascots. These mascots came in the form of Water Drop, Cloud, and Sun, and convey the message of simplicity, cleanness, and life. Decorating the walls of The Water Drop with bold facts about water, these mascots transform a space into a boutique. They act in the same way water itself does—they bring life to what otherwise could be dark, bland, and bleak.

Dinnick + Howells wanted to figure out a way to create a visual language that celebrated water, and the result was the mascots. This idea came to them because in The Water Drop, "water is the star." With a store dedicated entirely to water, what would make more sense than a design also dedicated entirely to water?

As it turns out, photographing something that is nearly invisible is a bit difficult. For one thing, under the camera the mascots would "act as mirrors to a certain degree and therefore catch lights and flare." Additionally, water seems to have a mind of its own. "Pure water is just too watery and wouldn't sit still for the camera," Jonathon Howell, creative director on the project, says. This was solved by adding sugar to the water, which helped it sit in place long enough to be photographed.

The Facts of the Matter

Once photographed, the mascots were placed on bottle labels and blown up to huge proportions on posters around the store. The personality-filled mascots are complemented by cold, hard facts about water. You know that 75 percent of one's brain is water, but did you know that even 22 percent of our bones are made up of water? You would find such facts in the store tucked around corners, behind doors, inside the filtration room, and in the washroom. Next in the works was a wonderful, encyclopedialike diagram that will explain the "path to purity" on the glass of the filtration room.

The end result is that the promotional graphics are so captivating that the store has been getting "compliments on the space and [finding] that the design of The Water Drop is very closely linked to people's return visits." Maybe the 75 percent of our brain filled with water is finally doing the thinking.

The store also wanted to be presented as the authority on clean water, a place where you can ask anything about it and get the answers. They sell bottled water, of course, but also coolers, home water filters, and other accessories. But it's all about water and nothing more.

Dinnick + Howells of Toronto, Canada, wanted to make this feel like a very different kind of boutique—sophisticated, smart, natural, but also friendly for the whole family.

How do you give a bottle of water personality? The design team created mascots in the form of Water Drop, Cloud, and Sun.

Design Firm stilradar

Client stilradar

Project 910 (a magazine for Stuttgart by stilradar)

A Brief History Lesson

Stuttgart, Germany—it's well known as a tourist center as well as a manufacturing center of electrical and photographic equipment, machinery, optical and precision instruments, textiles, clothing, chemicals, beer and wine, pianos, and motor vehicles. It's also known for having the highest per capita income of any German city. And it's also known for a funky little beautifully designed magazine known as *910*, produced courtesy of stilradar, a design firm.

The name *910* relates to the geographical coordinates of Stuttgart with 910 being the short term for 9°10' (9 degrees 10 minutes). The magazine is 60 pages long, each page measures 11" x 8½" (28 cm x 22 cm) and is produced in a limited edition run of 1,000. Anyone who is interested in the music, arts, lifestyle, fashion, architecture, and other happenings of Stuttgart can buy it at select shops throughout the town.

Featured here is the second edition of the magazine. The release is sporadic because it depends on the design firm's budget and time. But as with any self-promotion, the design firm tries to create time for the magazine because it showcases the designers' skills and gets the stilradar name known throughout the city.

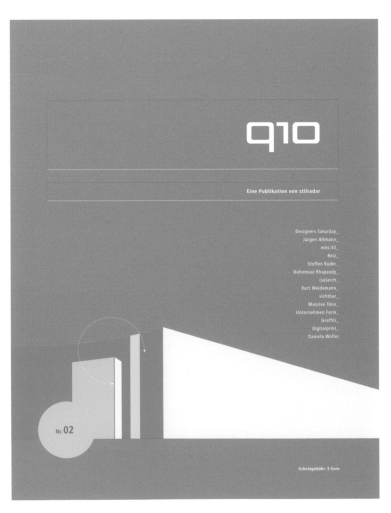

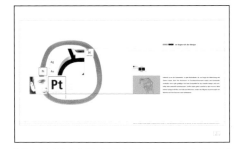

910 *is a promotional magazine designed by stilradar for Stuttgart, a German city with a significant design scene.*

Photography, illustration, and typography interact in surprising ways throughout the magazine, giving it a truly fresh feel and showing off the designers' capabilities.

Challenge Yourself

The *910* concept was the brainchild of Raphael Pohland and Simone Winter. They simply wanted to see if it was possible to push themselves to design and write an entire magazine. Each topic was different—they picked what was interesting to them personally, and so the topics include artists, musicians, and architects from Stuttgart. As Raphael explains it: "There was a wide range of not very well-known people but the articles in the magazine displayed them in a light that was exciting in contrast."

So *910* is a self-promotional magazine for the design firm, but it is also more than that. Raphael Pohland says: "It is our surroundings. People here are interested in these fields. The choice of the themes is subjective. For each edition we try to draw in a local photographer. They have full artist control and no restrictions. They can offer themes they are interested in and incorporate it into the magazine."

The second edition, shown here, was photographed by Jürgen Altmann. Raphael and Simone wrote nearly the whole magazine, from the first contact to the interviews to the articles. Besides the editorial work, they also did the design.

Visual Architecture

And the design is stunning. Type forms cityscapes. Photos and type interact in surprising ways. In the table of contents, for example, columns take the form of a cityscape. It is reminiscent of the way that Stuttgart as a city evolved. The center of the city, which formed its oldest part, was almost totally destroyed in World War II. After 1945, many old buildings were restored, and striking modern structures, such as the city hall and the concert hall, were erected.

As in the best of design, the design approach, the target audience, the content, and the surroundings all interact to form a whole that is greater than the sum of its parts.

The people gracing the pages of the magazine include a wide range of not very well-known people who are featured in unique ways.

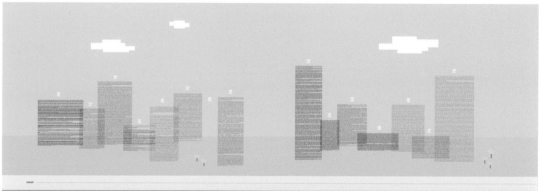

Stuttgart is the capital of the state Baden-Württemberg on the Neckar River. Here the typography treatment echoes the cityscape.

Tactile

Some promotions are designed to be touched. Some are made with unusual materials. Others are rendered in three dimensions when one would expect only two. Still others actively call out to the recipient to pick the piece up and interact with it. Whatever the method, the outcome is the same: these pieces say, "Please touch!"

Design Firm Kinetic Singapore

Client SingleTrek

Project Cannondale Headshok Bikes Poster Series

When Two Dimensions Aren't Enough

What better way to show the rugged terrain you might encounter on a mountain bike than with a series of posters that are actually three-dimensional? SingleTrek, a bike shop in Singapore, wanted to promote their Cannondale Headshok suspension mountain bikes. The strategy given to the design firm was single minded: find a unique and engaging way of demonstrating the capability of the new range of bike. So Kinetic, a local design firm, came up with a clever and unusual solution: to create a series of posters that each had its own 3-D paper sculpture depicting rugged terrain. According to Roy Poh, creative director, this let the audience "feel the action and show the true potential of the Headshok suspension mountain bikes"—a pretty impressive feat for something that doesn't use a word of copy.

No copy here. Just paper sculptures.

According to creative director Roy Poh, these posters let the audience "feel the action and see the true potential of the Headshok suspension mountain bikes."

Rough Roads Ahead

The client immediately gravitated to the concept, which created a classic case of *be careful what you wish fo*r. Roy and his creative partner, Pann Lim, then had to figure out a way to get it done. And because they had never created 3-D paper sculptures to be used on posters before, they didn't realize the numerous obstacles that would come up. There were problems with the thickness of the paper. First, it was too thick to create the perfect textures for the poster. Then, it was too thin to hold the poster together. After they finally determined the perfect thickness for the sculpture itself, they were chagrined to note that the poster kept becoming an odd shape after the textures were done. After much experimenting, the creative team arrived at the perfect solution. The trick, they discovered, was to use a much bigger piece of paper for the sculpture, create the texture, and then cut it down to size. The end result was 80 posters, each handmade and unique.

After much painstaking work, the response was all the creative team and client could have hoped for. The posters attracted a lot of attention, got people talking about the bikes, and the bike shop noted that the posters actually made people want to ride and feel the bikes on rough terrains.

Eighty of these posters were produced, and each one was handmade and unique.

Design Firm   Iridium, a design agency

Client   Genome Canada

Project   Promotion to Mark the Discovery of DNA

A Celebration of Science

A three-dimensional model of DNA pinned like a butterfly specimen to a poster. What better way to promote the fiftieth anniversary of the discovery of the DNA structure by Watson and Crick!

Genome Canada, a corporation funding genomics and proteomics research in Canada, wanted to mark the DNA anniversary in a notable way. They turned to Iridium of Ottawa, and asked them to get the attention of a target audience of federal government parliamentarians, health research—related agencies, scientific researchers, and academics.

A Touch of Creativity

The idea (reminiscent of scientists mounting exotic butterflies with pins) was certainly novel: no one had ever seen a poster that showcased the double helix as a natural specimen. Not to mention a poster in which the double helix has rivets holding it in place, as if the helix actually existed physically. It was an idea that immediately resonated with the target audience, who admired the innovation and understood what it was all about. In their eyes, the DNA molecule was treated as a true precious specimen from nature by mounting it on the poster. As in scientific research and laboratory protocol, the full scientific name was then applied to the poster on a simple white label. The poster was sent in a transparent

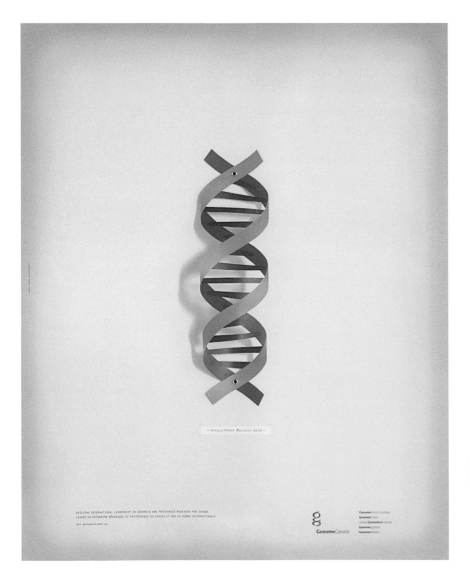

The double helix is actually a three-dimensional model, which is pinned to the poster like a butterfly specimen with metal rivets.

mailing tube echoing a test tube. Also included in the promotional package were a numbered, limited edition card, a bookmark, and a commemorative booklet that touches on the past, present, and future potential of the groundbreaking research being done by Genome Canada.

Finding clear plastic mailing tubes that resembled giant test tubes was no easy feat. Iridium finally was able to track them down from a California supplier. In another painstaking feat in honor of the DNA anniversary, the metal rivets on the poster had to be hand-applied because of the oversized sheet and required special handling and care. In total, 750 promotional packages were created.

The Crowd Cheers

Feedback was marvelous. People were pleased to receive a personalized package with a numbered limited edition card, a bookmark, and a commemorative booklet. This booklet was rather small in size as it had to be inserted into the mailing tube. All the pictures were printed on translucent paper stock, with the article by Watson and Crick published by the journal *Nature* in April 1953 serving as a colorful backdrop. On the cover of the booklet, on the tube, and on the bookmark, there is one simple word—extraordinary—where the letters d, n, and a are highlighted. This simple but effective play on words quickly resonated with the audience. Special box-framed versions of the poster were presented at a Genome Canada commemorative ceremony honoring their chairman and an academic head researcher. The overwhelming positive response from the enthusiastic audience created a rush for the posters from those in attendance. In fact, several requested that their posters be framed in the same display-style box frames as those presented.

All the promotional materials were packaged in clear plastic mailing tubes reminiscent of scientific test tubes.

On the cover of the booklet, on the tube, and on the bookmark, there is one simple word—extraordinary— where the letters d, n, and a are highlighted. According to art director Mario L'Écuyer, "This simple but effective play on words quickly found resonance with the audience."

Wake up and smell the coffee. Slow down, you're moving too fast. Relax, enjoy yourself. Go ahead, indulge. You're worth it.

As you age, you gain perspective. Certain things become easier than they ever were. Perhaps you're more secure in your job, or your children have grown. You seem to be more aware of how life works. You appreciate indulgences, feeling you've worked hard for them. Yet at the same time, there are definite physical signs of aging that need to be confronted. Your knees give out in bad weather, you don't sleep like you used to, you need to give in and get a pair of reading glasses. It's by no means impossible to keep up with life. But it does require a little extra effort.

First and foremost, marketing to the midlife group follows the rule of marketing to anyone: Talk to them as people. These are folks who have come into their own as individuals and who are reflecting on their life. If they are not content with the choices they've made thus far, they're in trouble.

For some purchase decisions, this is a group for whom brand loyalty may be firmly established, and there may be resistance to change. In fact, this is a group of people that often re-adopts brands from childhood. At the same time, they don't see themselves as totally inflexible either. They will try new things if the cues are in place that tell them, "This is something worthy of my time and energy, it is well made, well designed; this is something that's unique to me."

Design Firm   **Iridium, a design agency**

Client   **Iridium, a design agency**

Project   **Self-Promotional Giveaways**

To talk to the target audience in the 46- to 60-year-old age range, Iridium came up with the concept of a Power Nap Pillow.

What better product to give a hard-working older generation than their own custom-created blend of coffee?

Iridium, of Ottawa, Canada, wanted to send out promotional packages to people who had followed their career path and had entered the midlife age range. The people in this target group had successful jobs as group marketing and communications managers of high-tech and government agencies and were still very active with tight deadlines and hectic daily work schedules.

To talk to this group in a way that would feel unique to them, Iridium came up with the concept of a "Power Nap Pillow." This innovative product lets the target resuscitate their energy or reflect on personal burnout—not to mention that it offers the chance to take a discreet nap at their desks. The end result looks less like a promo item than a high-end product—and it comes complete with a 12-page guide on how to take time to rest.

Next, Iridium came out with their own brand of designer coffee, also to be given away to this target. Branded Big Dripper, it was delicious, custom-blended coffee, presented in its own custom-designed bags.

Iridium soon discovered that it wasn't talking to this group of people that was extraordinarily difficult, it was creating a custom coffee blend that people would actually like to drink that was challenging. Iridium studio staff became taste testers of various bean combinations for two weeks before the final Big Dripper blend (a mix of four different coffee beans) was settled upon.

Their target responded with widespread positive response to the fictitious coffee product. Many remarked: "I never heard of this coffee brand before, where can I get some?" Little did they know it was their first and last taste of Big Dripper.

While the design is detail-oriented and sophisticated, copy on the product itself takes a decidedly tongue-in-cheek approach. The coffee was called "radical designer coffee" that was "wind tunnel tested" and "DNA modified for ultimate caffeine wake-up power."

After all, although this group may be a bit older, they still have a sense of humor.

While the design is detail-oriented and sophisticated, copy on the product itself takes a decidedly tongue-in-cheek approach. After all, although this group may be a bit older, they still have a sense of humor.

Design Firm **Iron Design**
Client **Iron Design**
Project **Self-Promotion**

Safety Precautions

When designing a promotion involving flammable materials, please keep the following in mind:

1) Fireworks cannot be sent through the mail unless a designer doesn't mind designing from a jail cell.

2) Matches must always say "close cover before striking"—it's the law.

3) Regulators will not allow you to use coated two-sided stock for the cover, as they feel the matches might ignite coated stock on the inside of the matchbook, but not uncoated stock.

When Iron Design was founded 10 years ago, they got their start designing fun and irreverent packaging for the entertainment industry. Over the years, they've become more focused on branding and identity design, disciplines that demand a more sensitive aesthetic and maturity. Yet they've made an effort to hang on to their original directive to think outside the box and create design solutions that are charged with energy.

In the Event of Industry Stagnation . . .

On the other hand, the past several years have been depressing for the design business. So when it came time to do a much-needed self-promotional piece, Iron Design really wanted to wake up their audience up with a powerful, "let's start something" kind of a message. They definitely did not want this promo to be a static representation of their projects.

From concept to mailing the project took approximately 12 weeks to complete. As usual, self-promo pieces always get pushed to the back burner.

According to Todd Edmonds, creative director on the project, "The promotion gets great reactions from everyone who sees it. And the matches are a great leave-behind at restaurants, bars, clients, bowling alleys, police stations, mechanics shops, brothels, etc."

DESIGNS THAT STAND UP SPEAK OUT AND CANT BE IGNORED

. . . Think Creatively

What they did want was a vehicle that would allow the design firm to show off work to potential clients who have never heard of them, while making the promotional piece interactive, clever, and unique. Also, a 10-year anniversary was approaching, but Iron wasn't sure the message of "10 years old'" and "hire us" made sense in the same piece. So the idea evolved into custom matches. New contacts get the matchbooks with a mini portfolio inside. Existing clients receive the promo with the ten candles to remind them of Iron's history. The first thought was to send firecrackers along with the matches (see above for why they decided not to), but they settled on candles as a safer bet.

Boxes are recycled paper board jewelry boxes, insert cards are 1-color (metallic silver) on 100-pound dull-coated stock with die-cut slots for candles and matchbooks, 10 black candles are bundled together with red string (giving it that dynamite look), and matchbooks are custom designed.

Meeting Federal Regulations

Finding a vendor for the matchbooks took some research. Iron Design found a couple of vendors on the Web, requested samples, and finally chose Wagner Match in Colorado to produce the matches, based on the variety and quality of their work. Most of the high-end matches they produce are manufactured in Japan, where they can circumvent U.S. federal regulations—but it takes a month longer to complete them. Because Iron needed them in four weeks, they had to settle for U.S.—made matches. In the United States, all matches have to say "close cover before striking" and the matches must be made of cardstock with white tips. In Japan, a wide variety of match colors and tips are available and there's more latitude with matchbook cover text.

The match company assured Iron they could replace the "close cover before striking" line with "keep cover open—live dangerously," but the proof contained the standard saying. Iron decided to go with it for this round, and plans to produce future matches in Japan to allow more control. Live and learn. Next time they might try to live a little more dangerously. But hopefully they'll still stay out of jail.

Matches cost approximately $.16 each, boxes $.75, and cards and vellum about $1.50. An estimate of 600 matchbooks was sent out. Interns, as well as a staff assembly line, helped put them together.

Ten years in business: To celebrate, the recipient gets 10 black candles and a custom-designed matchbook complete with a mini portfolio.

The Flaming Iron: The latest representation of Iron Design—a "simple, colorful, hard-line graphic of a hot iron shooting off like a rocket [that's] easy to work with, representative of [Iron's] house style, and exciting."

Design Firm   Doppelganger, Inc.
Client   Doppelganger, Inc.
Project   Otto Cube

Drumroll, Please

In the running for the quickest, easiest, least expensive promotion ever, we present our top choice: The Otto Cube.

The promotion took exactly one day to conceptualize, design, produce, and ship out. There was not a single problem with production. No labored client meetings or rounds of revisions. And the promotion itself cost a mere $7.95 each.

Of course, it always helps when the designer and the client are one and the same.

Otto Steininger runs a small New York City illustration studio called Doppelganger. He has a simple, but effective philosophy: "Some people say illustration is all about the concept, but I believe it has to be visually intriguing in the first place—otherwise the viewer won't even get to appreciate the concept because he or she may have already overlooked the piece. And it has to work within split seconds."

The Otto Cube is an ingenious picture holder cleverly redesigned into a promotional vehicle for illustrator Otto Steininger.

Tech Specs

The Otto Cube is a 2" x 2" x 2" (5 cm x 5 cm x 5 cm) Plexiglas cube with a stainless steel backing on three sides that is commercially sold as a picture frame and has been customized by Otto. The original cube is manufactured by Umbra, Inc., designed by Tom Vincent, and is patented. Otto then created art that was printed on an Epson inkjet printer and trimmed, scored, and inserted by hand. It was packaged in a small cardboard box lined with silver tissue paper and sent out to a dozen key clients.

When You Least Expect It

The origin of the promotion was simple—lightning struck in an art supply store. Otto saw the cube and thought it would make an ideal promo vehicle. Because the cubes come with placeholder images, it was a quick jump to realize that his own illustrations would be infinitely more interesting than the placeholder images. So with a tone that mildly mocks the stereotypical baby or family pictures, he designed his own little placeholders. The copy reads: "Your baby picture here," "Your family picture here," and "My phone number here"; thus also mocking the fact that this is, in fact, a promo piece. But just so it was clear that Otto understood that people would ultimately want to add their own pictures in, he added a line in fine print that reads, "Please remove when tired of placeholder images."

The cubes were sent to clients with whom Otto had already established a relationship. Besides the fact that the Otto Cube was quick, easy, inexpensive, and painless to produce, what Otto likes most is the idea that it is usable beyond its promotional purpose. After all, recycling is good for everyone.

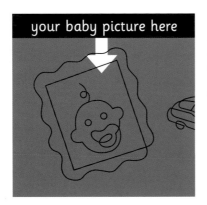

Otto's illustration style is fun, quirky, and iconic. Like any good brand, he is always looking for innovative ways to keep his name at the top of clients' minds.

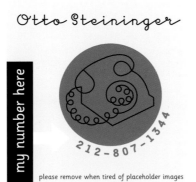

Of course, the illustrations are so cute that maybe people will continue to keep them in the cube. Or, even better, maybe they'll call Otto and ask for more.

Sensitive to the fact that people would ultimately prefer to have their own pictures of family, friends, or pets in the cube, Otto gives them permission to remove his illustrations with a small line of copy stating simply "Please remove when tired of placeholder images."

The Assignment

"The brief is on your desk. You need to design a holiday greeting card."

Two little sentences that are sure to strike fear into the heart of almost any designer.

The simple Christmas greeting can be one of the most challenging and tension-inducing briefs for a designer. You know it's coming at the same time, year after year, but finding yet another original, special, and festive idea seems almost impossible in the face of what's been done before.

The brief for this particular fear-inducing project was given to Bisqit Design for Hill & Knowlton UK, part of a global PR consultancy with a broad industry sector base. The brief said that the card needed to be able to be sent from both corporate and consumer divisions, and it should be multinational with no distinct religious or cultural bias. It was being sent out to clients worldwide—about 3,500 total.

As it happened, Bisqit Design had three briefs for Christmas cards going at the time and had been experimenting with stand-up trees and folds and die-cuts. The design firm went through two concept stages for this card, without any ideas catching the imagination or fully meeting the brief. So they returned to the simplicity of the materials, print processes, and die-cuts. Reconsidering how a tree could be realized as a die-cut from a different perspective produced an impressive result. The finishing touches of the gloss one-side "white Christmas" and uncoated one-side "green Christmas" flowed immediately. Like many solutions, it looks a lot simpler than the process from which it evolved.

The client originally asked for their logo to be printed on the card, but when it came time to consider the type and text greeting, it was obvious that the full-color logo would detract from the simple effect of the tree scenes. Bisqit recommended the understated typography and spelled out the company name as a more sympathetic approach to the overall design.

DESIGNS THAT STAND UP SPEAK OUT AND CANT BE IGNORED

126

Card Specifications

The resulting card is 8¼" x 6" (21 cm x 15 cm), printed on Chromolux 700 (coated one side), matched green one side, silver print both sides, and was mailed in an Exposé pearlescent envelope.

Because of the very short lead time for production, Bisqit knew they wouldn't be able to laser-cut the trees, making the less forgiving die-cutting technique the only option. They wanted to maintain a simple elegance and curvaceous quality in the tree outlines, so they worked closely with the finishing company to make sure the small turns and curves of the trees could be achieved in the metal cutter. A few back-and-forths with PDF die-cut outlines and folds that wouldn't crack when creased, and they hit upon the final design solution.

Now Everyone Wants One

The card was designed and produced for the United Kingdom office of Hill & Knowlton, but when other offices saw the card, they wanted it, too, including the worldwide CEO of Hill & Knowlton based in New York City. The print run of 3,500 was quickly depleted as people scrambled to get their hands on some. Bisqit was asked to a do a reprint, but it would not have been delivered by Christmas. Many recipients called and expressed their delight at being able to send out such a surprising, elegant card to their clients.

Now the question arises: "What in the world are we going to do for *next* year?"

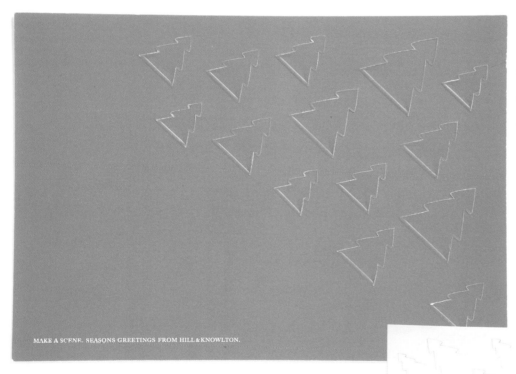

Bisqit designed this holiday card for PR firm Hill & Knowlton UK. From the agreed design route through testing to delivery took about two weeks; design and tests took five days; and printing and finishing took five days.

Bisqit Design's philosophy: "We start with the expectation that something great is what we will achieve. Brave clients, forgiving deadlines and budgets, unexpected moments of inspiration, paper, and the desire to always try again if it isn't quite working are just a few of the potential contributors to success."

Interactive

Although most of the promotions in this category are Web-based, we really mean "interactive" in every sense of the word. Each promotion in this category is designed to require some sort of involvement with the target audience. Not always an easy task, but the best interactive promotions do this to a tee.

Design Firm	**Origin**
Client	**Claire Monaghan**
Project	**Business Card**

Okay, tough guy. You want your own personal fitness instructor? First you'll have to pass the all-important test—being strong enough to open the business card.

That's right. No need to read that sentence again. This is a business card that is actually designed so that it takes sheer physical strength to get at the information.

A "Tough" Client

Self-employed personal fitness instructor Claire Monaghan was looking for a business card and letterhead that would make her memorable among all the other fitness instructors around the Cheshire-area gyms in the United Kingdom. The plain white cards that you could do yourself at a copy shop just weren't for her. She knew that she might be the expert on personal fitness training, but she was no design guru.

Enter Origin.

It looks like an ordinary business card, albeit in a bright, contemporary color scheme. But, wait, there's no information on the outside . . .

. . . and it takes brute strength to open it up to get the information. Perhaps because you need a personal fitness trainer?

DESIGNS THAT STAND UP SPEAK OUT AND CANT BE IGNORED

128

A small design firm in the United Kingdom, Origin jumped at the chance to do something that would solve a unique problem. Origin has on its roster big names like Bentley Motors, Rolls-Royce, and Coca-Cola, but there's nothing like a unique design challenge to get the creative juices flowing. In fact, the design firm states as part of their credo on their website: "If you're looking for design with an agency house style, ideas initiated by computer, the latest marketing jargon, then maybe you shouldn't stop here. That's not what Origin is about. If on the other hand you want designers who you can talk to intelligently about strategy and brief, who are talented and commercial enough to create work that excites them, excites you, and impacts your brand then please continue."

So when a client who wants something exciting meets with a design firm who wants to make it exciting, guess what the results are? Monaghan came to the design firm knowing she wanted a card with an overall look that was contemporary as well as unique. The clientele she was going after were young professionals who were active and hip. The rest she left to Adam Lee, designer at Origin.

By Design, a Card That's Hard to Open

From the very start of the project, Lee felt it would be appropriate for the stationery to be physically difficult to open; it was just a question of how. All the creative challenges in this case were mental, not physical. The solution was simple and elegant. By doubling the pages of a four-page card and folding them inside itself, the elastic band could be hidden from the viewer until they tried to open it. A similar method of thinking was applied to the letterhead. A perforated strip was added to the bottom and then stuck into the base of an A4 envelope. The result is that the recipient of the letterhead would have to apply quite an effort to separate the letterhead from the glued strip when pulling it out of the envelope. For both pieces, a contemporary look was achieved by using cool colors and large text in a clean sans serif font.

The Claire Monaghan stationery won a Commendation at the 2002 Roses Design Awards and was also nominated for a Cream Award in the same year. And people all around the health clubs of the United Kingdom are stronger from it.

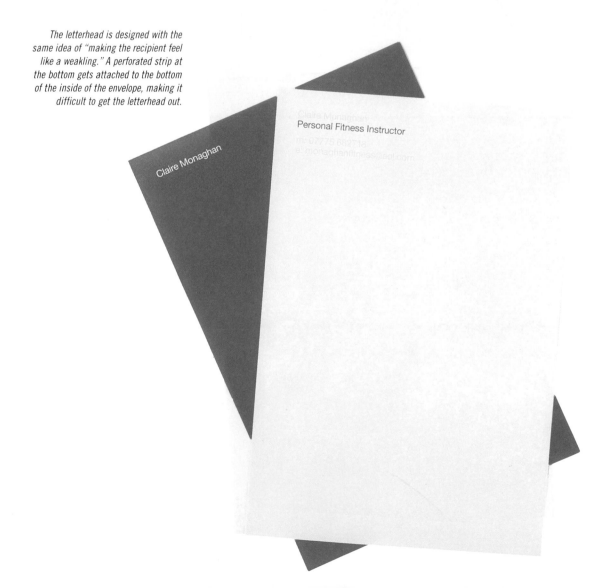

The letterhead is designed with the same idea of "making the recipient feel like a weakling." A perforated strip at the bottom gets attached to the bottom of the inside of the envelope, making it difficult to get the letterhead out.

Design Firm **Double You**

Client **Diesel International**

Project **Online Promotion**

Instructions for Destruction

Imagine a promotion where you are told you had to smash your keyboard in order to participate. That's exactly what visitors to the online promotion for Diesel International were told to do.

The site was designed by Double You, in Barcelona, Spain. It's all part of Diesel International's campaign "Action for Successful Living." And how does one live more successfully? As copy on the website states, "If you want to live a successful life, you have to fight for it. Shout. This is a wake-up call for the rebel inside you." The Diesel advertising campaign was telling people to stand up, join together, and clamor for those things that could help them to get to more successful living—write more love letters, kiss your neighbors, free every goldfish, help create a world with more green traffic lights, and four-day weekends, for starters.

Double You, of Barcelona, Spain, was charged with creating a microsite under the brand of Diesel International's "Action for Successful Living."

Diesel's interactive website is all about rebellion and the fight for life. In fact, it encourages users to break their keyboards—something Double You actually admitted to doing during site testing.

A visitor to the site soon discovers that smashing the keyboard or shouting at the computer's microphone is the only way to navigate around the site.

Leading an Interactive Rebellion . . .

So Double You was charged with creating a microsite within Diesel's main site, one that would provide a type of interactive training for trendy demonstrators who wanted to voice their rebellion. The aim was to involve people in an unexpected and "out of the box" Diesel interactive experience built around the concept of "Action for Successful Living." Double You knew that what they wanted most was to provoke a strong physical interaction between the users and the microsite. The birth of the idea came during a passionate group brainstorming session where the designers were discussing how to make that happen. Suddenly someone said, "In riots people shout and smash things." Bingo! Let's smash the keyboard! As a user soon discovers, smashing the keyboard or shouting at the computer's microphone is the only way to navigate around the site. And it's certainly one way to "experience successful living," especially for the core target audience of boys and girls ages 17 and 30. This is a group that likes to be surprised. And the site does that by providing a new way of experiencing a website.

. . . Can Be Rewarding

Although it might usually be difficult to sell a promotional idea that incites people to smash their keyboards, in this case, Diesel expected the agency to come back with something like that. The end result is a site that has been one of the most-awarded Diesel advertising action sites in 2002 and 2003. The agency credits the success of the campaign with its guiding philosophy of keeping it simple, creating a dialogue with users, and improving the power of interactivity. And they also admit that they broke two keyboards during the first testing of the site.

The Diesel advertising campaign was telling people to stand up, join together, and take action for successful living—write more love letters, kiss your neighbors, free every goldfish, help create a world with more green traffic lights, and four-day weekends, for starters.

According to Diesel International, "If you want to live a successful life, you have to fight for it. Shout. This is a wake-up call for the rebel inside you."

The target audience is boys and girls ages 17 and 30, a group that likes to be surprised.

Design Firm **Double You**

Client **Seat**

Project **León Cupra R Promotional Campaign**

A Speedy Call to Action

Step on the accelerator. With those simple words, an online promotion for León Cupra R, the fastest and most powerful car ever made by Seat, was born.

The idea came from Double You, a design firm in Barcelona, Spain. Double You has an agency philosophy that vows to "keep improving the power of interactivity." They certainly seem to be succeeding, as indicated by this bit of press: "For the first time in the history of the San Sebastian Festival an interactive agency is awarded as Agency of the Year." And that recognition was at least in part due to their work for Seat's León Cupra R automobile.

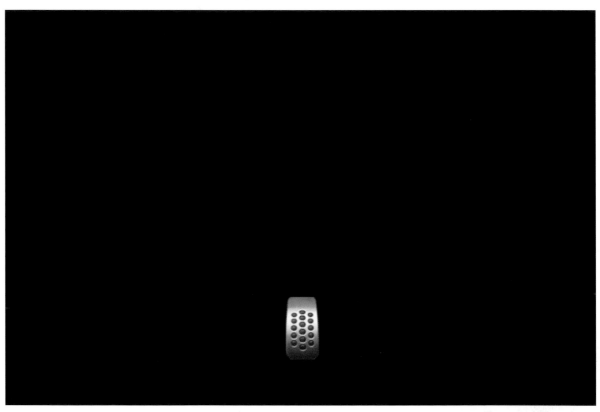

Are you ready? Then go ahead and step on the accelerator.

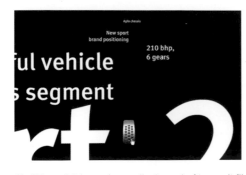

You'll immediately experience a dizzying rush of type as it flies at you. Blink, and you'll miss what's being said. But no matter. Words just can't equal the feeling of acceleration.

Talk Is Cheap

Double You knew they wanted to make the online experience for potential car buyers a visceral one. They wanted to make the user experience the power and speed of the sports car, rather than just tell them about it.

As Fredo puts it, "We were obsessed with the idea of a site that could make users feel the sensation of speed and power without any kind of blah-blah. We wanted something they could easily experience by themselves. When the team was talking about the first thing you want to do when you test a real sports car everybody agrees on one thing: step on the accelerator."

So take a client who was enthusiastic from the get-go, and combine it with a target audience of middle-class men between the ages of 20 and 30 who enjoy sporty cars. The result is a *The Fast and the Furious*–type experience on the web. A simple iconic accelerator pedal soon turns into a dizzying rush of type flying at the viewer. Blink, and you'll miss what's being said. But no matter. Words just can't equal the feeling of acceleration. The experience is equal to the feeling of pressing the gas pedal of a 210-horsepower Seat Cupra R, with its power and head-spinning speed. Only at the end of the journey is a picture of the car and readable information actually revealed.

The Finish Line

Not only does the target audience enjoy the online experience, but the Cupra R, Sport FR, and Sports Limited models have become the bestsellers of Seat's Leónrange. The promotion has won many awards, and even though it was designed only for the website in Spain, Seat Mexico bought the site for the Mexican market.

Are you ready? Then go ahead and step on the accelerator.

Only at the end of the journey is a picture of the car and readable information actually revealed.

New SEAT León Cupra R

more information at www.seat.es

Fun with Words

First of all, you've got to love the name. Bluecashew is a PR and event production agency, and its name is a play on the name of the founder, Sean Nutley. And with a name so cool and sophisticated, they needed a way of promoting themselves online that would do the name justice.

Design firm deepend was called in to establish bluecashew as a premier player in the world of public relations and event production. An online presence was needed to create a coherent and seamless identity program that elevates the company a notch above their competitors. And yes, deepend helped with the name generation as well.

The conceptual idea of the site was to show how bluecashew works hard for you "behind the scenes." One of the most graphic ways of showcasing that idea is through the sliding doors, which open and close to reveal layers of type, information, and illustrations. The illustrations—with a charming whimsy that's part fashion, part art—add to the behind the scenes concept by allowing the people depicted to remain faceless yet somehow imbued with personality. The combined result is a format that allows the dynamic events and promotions organized by bluecashew to be showcased without needing to be overly specific.

The sophistication and elegance of the execution speaks volumes in a marketplace where the competition can come across as being too corporate or not trendy. It seems particularly appropriate for a target audience composed of higher level decision-making executives in the industries of fashion, media and communications, marketing, art and design, publishing, and benefits.

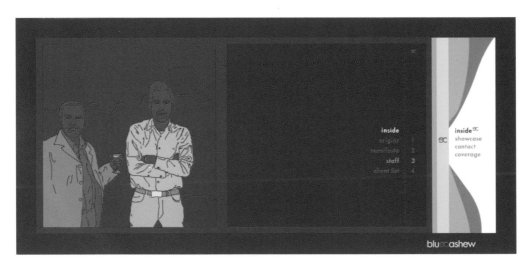

Bluecashew is a PR and event production agency, and its name is a play on the name of the founder, Sean Nutley. And with a name so cool and sophisticated, they needed a way of promoting themselves online that would do the name justice.

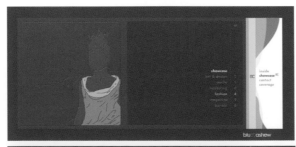

The conceptual idea of the site was to show how bluecashew works hard for you behind the scenes. One of the most graphic ways of showcasing that idea is through the sliding doors, which open and close to reveal layers of type, information, and illustrations.

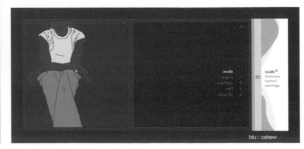

Everything's Symbolic

Because details are everything in design, one small one seems worth pointing out. Deepend chose to make an icon out of the letters ec—the bridge between the word *blue* and the word *cashew*. This ec icon was designed to function similarly to the © or ® symbol, in which it could be placed after a client's name. This device helps to reinforce the behind the scenes aspect of the brand concept.

The illustrations were created by one of the in-house designers, and they came about from the notion that the company needed to create a stylized way to portray what bluecashew does without getting too specific. It helps that the illustrations give it a unique look, a look that communicates the brand's essence in an elegant and sophisticated manner.

And it is certainly befitting a company with the name of bluecashew.

It helps that the illustrations give it a unique look, a look that communicates the brand's essence in an elegant and sophisticated manner.

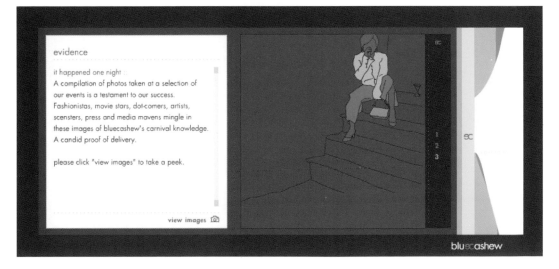

Memo to self: Lose weight. Stop smoking. Save money. Every year around this time that little voice enters our head. We may not give it much regard, but it's in there. The voice that tells us to face our future this year with resolve.

And so starts this lovely little booklet of New Year's resolutions, sent out as a promo piece by IE Design. But it's New Year's resolutions with a twist, or should we say a flip? The piece is actually a miniature flip book with which readers interact to form their own New Year's resolutions, which are surprising and inspiring.

Trust Your Wardrobe

Every year, IE Design produces an extravagant holiday mailing for friends, clients, and contacts. The piece serves not only as a promotion for the studio, but as a creative release for the design team—a showcase of the design firm's talents. For this year in particular, they wanted the mailing to be "poignant and thoughtful, but still depict a bit of wit and playfulness," according to Marcie Carson, project designer.

Question the Government

The small format (3½" x 4¾" [9 cm x 12 cm]) and die-cut pages allow the reader to flip through the book to create an array of New Year's resolution combinations. These permutations cover the spectrum, from "Stop—Fingernail Biting" to "Love—The Neighbor's Dog" to "Celebrate—Your Family." The best thing about it is that the reader gets to create messages that are uniquely personal.

IE Design's promotional holiday booklet titled "Re:Solutions" successfully addresses the many emotions associated with the holiday season.

Forgive Your Car

The target audience is particularly diverse, so it was important that the language and image selection appealed to most anyone. The word choices and corresponding photos took a long time to select, especially since the designers were working on a very tight budget and only wanted to use images from their existing royalty-free library.

Focus on Your Family

In the end, this elegant concept complemented the format. As Carson puts it, "It's one of those times that form and function meld together perfectly."

Celebrate the Neighbor's Dog

Each year IE Design receives numerous phone calls and email messages regarding their holiday mailings. Although it's not clear if an awarded project is a direct result of the holiday mailing, it's still a great way to keep creativity in front of clients.

Memo to self: Do what you are able. And always, always remember to take time out to enjoy. Happy holidays from the friendly folks at IE Design.

It's New Year's resolutions with a twist—a flip of the hand and an almost infinite number of funny, poignant, and quirky resolutions can be created.

Design Firm Dotzero Design
Client Dotzero Design
Project Invitation and T-Shirt

"Come one, come all! Gather 'round and see the Dotzero crew with your own eyes—prepare to be amazed and astonished! Anyone with a ticket is guaranteed to walk away with a prize!"

Sounds like something a sleazy carnival guy would say, right? Well, don't worry, this promotion has nothing to do with circuses or carnivals—although there is a giant fish involved, but we'll get to that later. For now, let's talk about parties.

Time to Celebrate

Dotzero, a Portland, Oregon–based graphic design outfit, had just relocated to a new office, and it was time for a party. To promote the open house, they wanted to design a piece that could serve as both an invitation and an announcement, as well as create T-shirts to hand out on the night of the event. Their target audience included friends and family members of the Dotzero community and other designers in the field. Of course, the design firm called upon their own creative team for this project; why hire someone else when the most qualified people for the job are in house?

Announcing the Open House

The front of the invitation was heavy on earth tones—it was composed mainly of browns and tans—and featured a sequence of shots that showed the location of the office. Each frame brought the viewer progressively closer to Dotzero's headquarters; the first shot was a distant view of the building, the next one was of the lobby entrance, and so on.

The flip side read, "Our mothers have always said, why don't you move out of the house? So, we did. Announcing our new office right above Mother's (Bistro)." Jon Wippich, the creative director at Dotzero, explains that Mother's Bistro is a sort of landmark in the area, so they decided to work it into the copy in a creative and humorous way.

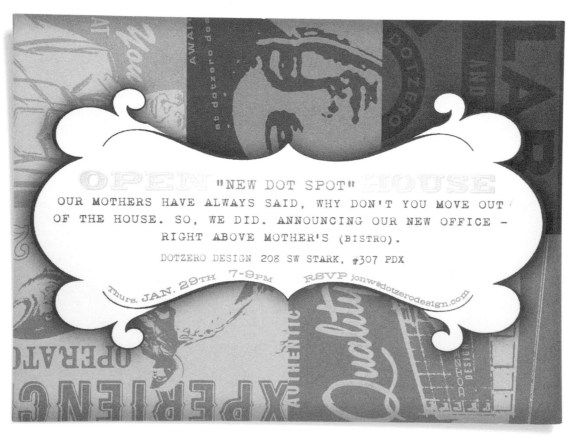

The folks at Dotzero had just relocated to a new office and set out to design an invitation promoting their open house.

The final component of the invitation was a ticket to the open house. It was attached to the actual invitation, adding an element of tactility and interactivity. The ticket resembled an old-fashioned movie pass and carried more humorous copy: "Come topless if you want. Or not. We'll give you a free T-shirt to wear home. Bring this ticket and select from five different designs."

Something to Take Home

The second half of Dotzero's open house preparations involved churning out five T-shirt designs for the event. One of those T-shirts showed a man riding on the back of a giant fish. Its copy read, "Experienced operators." Another T-shirt announced, "Authentic quality design since several years ago!" And although each of the T-shirts was different, they all had a vintage, retro feel about them, with slogans reminiscent of old print advertisements.

A Challenging Business

Dotzero encountered some slight pratfalls, er, obstacles and challenges in the production stage. Wippich recalls they had to determine which ink palettes were best suited for which fabric colors—and, as an added complication, women's shirts came in different colors than the men's. As for the invite, the creative team originally wanted the ticket to resemble a postage stamp, with a rough, staggered edge—but that was too pricey. Wippich explains, "We changed the design to be more like a movie ticket, with the quarter circles cut on the corners."

Phew! Life under the creative big top can certainly be unpredictable. Thankfully, there were no reported cases of elephant tramplings.

The old-fashioned movie tickets added an element of tactility and interactivity to the open house invitations.

The creative team designed several T-shirts for the open house to hand out as giveaways— and although each one showed off a unique graphic, all the designs had a vintage, retro feel.

How do you come up with a great design concept when there's simply no time to do so? Kai Clemen of Wasserman & Partners explains how they did it: "We came up with the idea somewhere between ummmm and errr."

Whistler Blackcomb Mountain (WB) was experiencing a shortfall in holiday bookings at many of the major hotel and accommodation destinations. To kickstart bookings, WB asked Wasserman to create an online viral campaign to drive people to book online.

There's No Time Like the Present

The request was simple: come up with something clever, funny, and simple, something people would forward to their friends. There was only one snag; the project had to be completed immediately. The Web ad needed to be up and running within the week.

With such little notice the folks at Wasserman quickly realized they would need to talk to a local market—people who could take advantage of the deal now. And those people, they found, tended to avoid Whistler Blackcomb because they perceived it to be overcrowded and way too expensive. So Wasserman had to adjust that perception and tell people there was plenty of room available at a great price.

"Hello, hello, can you hear me? You just got knocked out. Next time, wear a helmet."

Wasserman & Partners in Vancouver, Canada, wanted to illustrate how much kick-ass air time you can get at Whistler Blackcomb.

The limited time frame meant the production had to be very simple. With little time and money, the design firm decided to illustrate the piece, which helped give it a young and comic feel. They wanted it to be irreverent to appeal to the local markets' cynical perception of tourists cluttering around their mountain. Plus, Clemen adds, "it made us laugh, and that's always a good sign."

With the clock ticking, they had a local Flash artist record his voice to create some hilarious, low-budget sound effects for the cursor icons. It gave the piece that extra kick for talk value and encouraged users to pass the URL along to one friend, and then another, and another.

A Rush Project Has Benefits All Its Own

The good thing about such a speedy turnaround time is that things just have to happen to stay on schedule. There were no production issues, no time for client revisions, and no time to overthink it. All in all, it took about two days to conceptualize, two days to execute, and one day to approve.

To tell people that helmet rentals were available, we get the view from someone just recovering consciousness. The second was designed to promote how "kick ass" Whistler Blackcomb's terrain park is, how much air time you can get, and basically how cool it is. The promo shows a snowboarder doing a trick in the air—and the view is from inside an airplane cockpit. "Young kids like that sort of stuff," says Clemen nonchalantly. Two stock images from Getty pictures were combined to create the simple effects. The ad is just a neat and simple idea, which is what most ads should be.

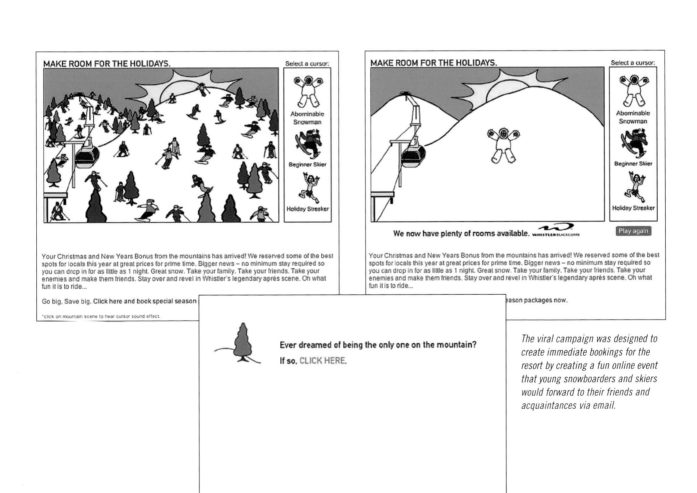

The viral campaign was designed to create immediate bookings for the resort by creating a fun online event that young snowboarders and skiers would forward to their friends and acquaintances via email.

Design Firm Nesnadny + Schwartz

Client International Spy Museum

Project Website

Spies Like Us

Espionage is a funny thing. Its fantasy and reality are so blurred that we don't even know where to draw the line. There are so many spy movies, so many tall tales about spies from all over the world, and so many spy jokes and gadgets and clichés, but what do we really know about the profession?

The International Spy Museum tries to crack some of these codes (no pun intended). The Museum is impressive not only for what it contains but also because it is "the first museum in the United States solely dedicated to espionage" and the only one in the world that provides a global perspective of this secretive profession, a profession that has shaped history and continues to influence world events. As the website proudly proclaims, "The International Spy Museum features the largest collection of international spy-related artifacts ever placed on public display. The stories of individual spies, told through film, interactives, and state-of-the-art exhibits provide a dynamic context to foster an understanding of espionage and its impact." Founder and chairman Milton Maltz adds, "The International Spy Museum is more than history—more than information or entertainment—its mission is to reflect the significance of intelligence as a critical component of national security."

Wow! Heavy stuff. But it's also . . . well . . . fun.

The problem with designing a website for something that's so monumental is that you have a lot to live up to. That was the challenge faced by design firm Nesnadny + Schwartz when they were hired by the International Spy Museum to create their website.

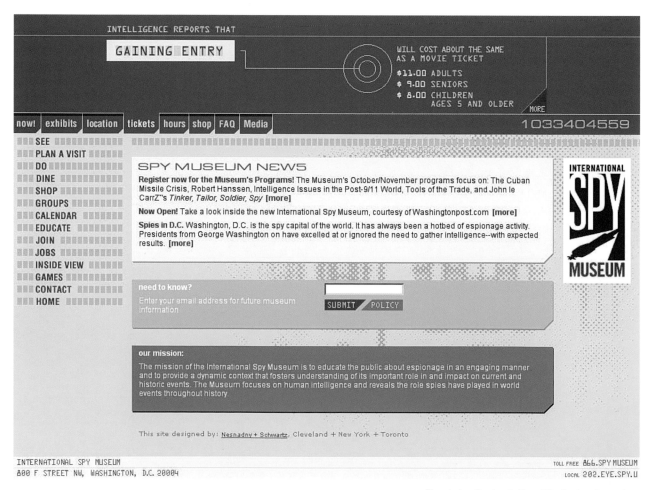

The mission: To educate the public about espionage in an engaging manner and to foster an understanding on the importance of espionage on current and historic events.

Mission, Accomplished

To start this mission, Nesnadny + Schwartz determined what they wanted the website to accomplish. These goals included: create a valuable tool for multiple audiences; create awareness; give attendees and the media a visual hook; introduce the new logo and brand efficiently; and provide users with up-to-date news, games, and a countdown clock for the grand opening of the museum. They also posed the challenge to themselves to make the website "historical, yet contemporary; simple, yet iconographic, as well as memorable." As the process began, Nesnadny + Schwartz made sure to keep the design for the Spy Museum's logos, brochures, and website all the same to create a unity between all forms of design for the museum. The project took six months to complete.

As you sign on to the website, you feel excited immediately, as you are told that your mission is to "gather information and discover secrets." If you answer "yes" to the question "Do you accept?" then you are let past the introductory page. When users visit the site, they can "cover, break codes, identify disguised spies, and become subjects of covert surveillance throughout their visit."

So sit yourself down, pour yourself a martini—shaken, not stirred—and become a spy for a day from the safety of your own home.

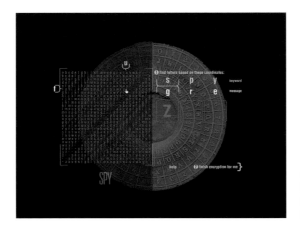

An elaborate secret code allows visitors to the site a way to compose encrypted messages and send them to a friend.

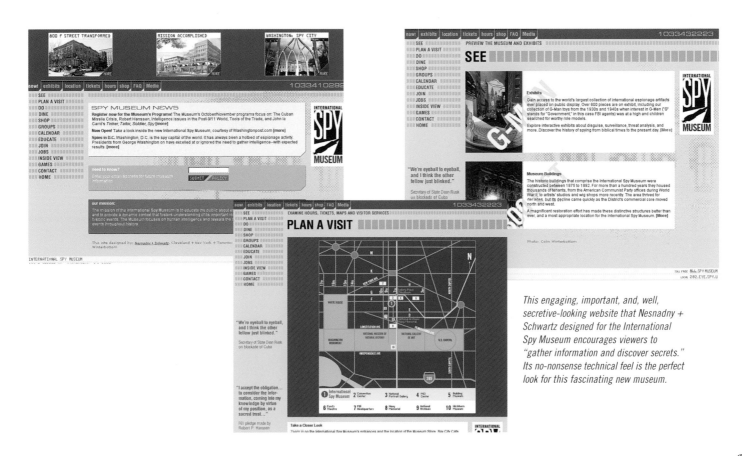

This engaging, important, and, well, secretive-looking website that Nesnadny + Schwartz designed for the International Spy Museum encourages viewers to "gather information and discover secrets." Its no-nonsense technical feel is the perfect look for this fascinating new museum.

"You are the weakest link. Got it? And wait, there's more—you don't know Jack!"

A New Technology, A New Kind of Promotion

Tune in to a modern game show, and you're guaranteed to sharpen your tongue by picking up a handy new phrase or two for your arsenal of verbal insults. But just how sharp are your listening skills? Well, there's a game for that, too—you can test out your aural acuity by playing ScanSoft's Speechify Challenge.

Jack Morton Worldwide, a New York City marketing firm, created the interactive Flash-based game as a promotion for Speechify, a product of ScanSoft. In brief, it was a new text-to-speech (TTS) technology that converted strings of text into natural-sounding human voices. Although Speechify wasn't the first computerized speech engine to hit the market, it was able to simulate inflections more accurately and convincingly than its predecessors.

Getting Down to Business

However, ScanSoft's new TTS engine wasn't developed merely for entertainment purposes; it was, in fact, designed specifically for professional use. Anya Beaupre, the producer of brand marketing at Jack Morton, explains, "The target audience consisted of clients that ScanSoft believed would have the greatest need for text-to-speech technology—virtually any business with a large portion of its customer base calling in for automated information, such as airlines, banks, and credit card companies."

The Speechify Challenge is an interactive, Flash-based game that Jack Morton Worldwide created to promote ScanSoft's new text-to-speech technology.

Jack Morton adopted a game show format for their promotion as a way to engage users while educating them on the capabilities of Speechify.

The game is elegantly simplistic, even in its color scheme—black, orange, and blue were the only colors used.

Take a Game Break

Jack Morton decided to adopt a game show format for ScanSoft's interactive promotion as a way to engage clients while educating them on the capabilities of Speechify. Potential clients were encouraged to visit the site and play the game: for each of six multiple-choice questions, players would first hear a sound bite, then decide whether it was a text-to-speech voice or a real human voice. As a bonus feature, users could sample a clip demonstrating Speechify's capabilities at work in their specific business or industry, but they had to finish the game first!

From a graphic standpoint, the game's design was elegantly simple; the only colors used were black, orange, and blue. And instead of live photography, Jack Morton used all digital artwork. Incidentally, this project was their first in which all the digital video they shot would later be converted into Macromedia Flash. The host of the Speechify Challenge, although a mere silhouette, was realistically rendered. That unique visual element, in combination with the modest use of color, resulted in a somewhat mysterious, yet alluring, user interface.

The Good News First

Because all game scores were recorded into a database, ScanSoft was able to track players' success in distinguishing real voices from digitized ones. On average, they found, people only responded correctly to about three or four of the six questions. As Beaupre concludes, "Most people still couldn't tell the difference between a text-to-speech voice and a human one—good news for ScanSoft."

It's a shame the Speechify Challenge wasn't a certified hearing test—then, it would have been great news for ear doctors, too.

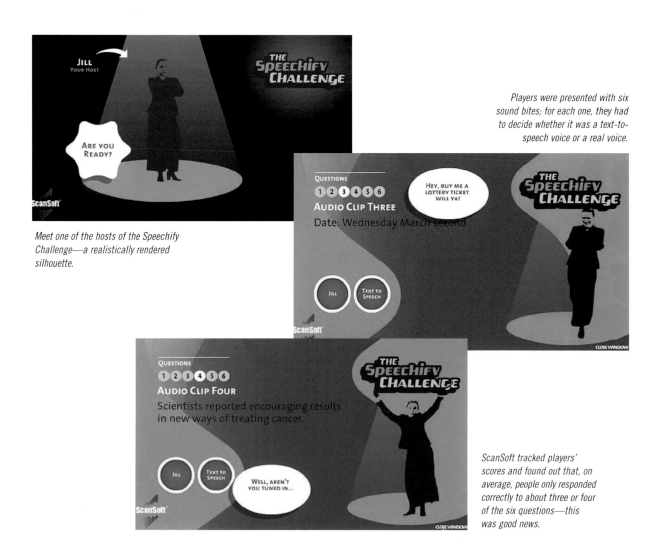

Players were presented with six sound bites; for each one, they had to decide whether it was a text-to-speech voice or a real voice.

Meet one of the hosts of the Speechify Challenge—a realistically rendered silhouette.

ScanSoft tracked players' scores and found out that, on average, people only responded correctly to about three or four of the six questions—this was good news.

A Perfect Circle

The perfect circle. Throughout the ages, the circle has been a highly symbolic and almost mystical shape. And it's also the perfect symbol for an innovative promotional piece designed to show off a 360-degree virtual tour.

Kolegram is a design firm in Canada. Headlight is a photography studio. Together, they wanted to send out a promotional piece that would tell people they were partnering up to provide 360-degree motion photography to those who wanted it. The package was sent to potential clients—those most likely to have a need for the sophisticated photography and those that would benefit from 3-D Web display of their product or service. Organizations such as museums, tourist attractions, parks, and clients in the automobile, retail, and technology industries were the target market.

The bubble-wrap envelope is just the beginning of this intriguing package.

The piece is a self-promotion for Kolegram (a design firm) and Headlight (a photography studio). Headlight produces the virtual tours for clients and Kolegram produces all the design elements.

Interesting Even Before It's Opened

The piece is interesting from the moment it arrives in the mail because it is packed in a bubble-wrap envelope that allows the design to peek through. Bubble wrap, as you may know, is inherently funny. The designers had immediately made a choice that was part design, part functional—the bubble wrap protected the actual CD-ROM enclosed in the mailing process, but it also looked intriguing. Upon opening up the envelope, the recipient sees a cute 1950s-style robot and green pixels. The pixel is a nice design element, but according to Mike Teixeira, creative director on the project, it also signified the birth of the original idea. They wanted to show that it all starts with a pixel and then ultimately a 360-degree virtual tour is born. The idea comes to life as the recipient continues the unfolding process and the piece ends with a perfect circle. A flat, panoramic view of 360 photography graces the outer edge, with an actual CD-ROM sitting snugly in the middle. The CD gives a demo of the actual tour. As the copy states, "Visitors are immersed in authenticity; the result, a genuine comprehension of your environment or product."

A Few Small Headaches

Producing the piece had its share of headaches. First, a glitch occurred in the folding process. The designers found that the thickness of the paper combined with the unusual task of folding something that's final flat shape would be a circle meant that it was difficult to get a nice, neat, flat folded piece. A double line score fixed it.

Another interesting thing about the production process is that once the round shaped die cut was done, there were left-over bits of paper along the edges. The only way to clean the edges was by paper sanding it.

Not so easy to form a perfect circle after all. No wonder it's so symbolic.

This piece is appealing because of its unusual die cut. It forms a perfect circle, which is a visual way to show the three-dimensional environment on a two-dimensional piece of paper.

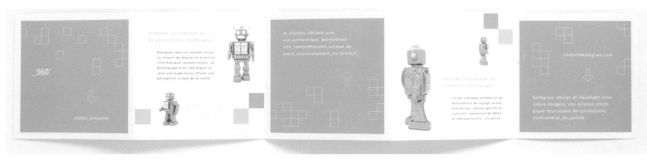

The reaction to the promotion was very good but due to virtual tour production costs, the market wasn't ready to jump in yet.

Design Firm **Design Guys**

Client **Willey House**

Project **Frank Lloyd Wright Website**

Universal Wisdom

"Form follows function—that has been misunderstood. Form and function should be one, joined in a spiritual union."

Those were the wise words of Frank Lloyd Wright, master architect of the late nineteenth and early twentieth centuries. Although it's safe to assume he was describing his technique as an architect, his philosophy is an important one to consider even outside the realm of blueprinting. And it's not just a coincidence that some of the best promotional tools employ this exact methodology.

How to Promote a Restoration Effort

Which brings us to Minneapolis, Minnesota—home of the Design Guys and the Willey House. The former is a design firm that provides its clients with a wide range of services, including branding, advertising, product development, and website design. The latter is Wright's 1934 creation for a client by the name of Malcolm Willey.

But what do the two have in common? Design Guys purchased Wright's creation in 2002 with plans to restore it. Shortly afterward, the Minneapolis design firm put their own architectural expertise to use and created a website detailing their recent acquisition.

Potential visitors to the website include Wright enthusiasts, historians, architects, and students. Art director Steve Sikora explains, "The purpose of the site is to inform to almost any degree the visitor is willing to go." And, as there had been both local and national concern surrounding the preservation of the house, the site effectively assured visitors that the house would be properly rescued. To invite traffic, the site was linked to numerous other Frank Lloyd Wright websites, and its URL was included with stories published on the Willey House.

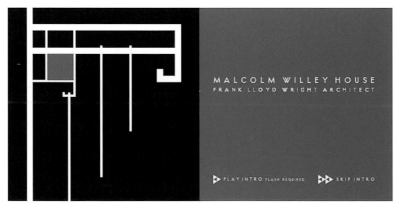

Visitors to the website include Wright enthusiasts, historians, architects, and students.

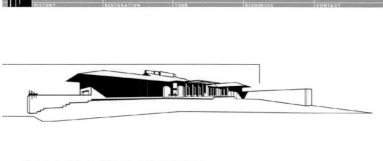

The site's elegance and simplicity make it unmistakable to users that they have stumbled across Frank Lloyd Wright in cyberspace.

Site Architecture

One of the most effective design elements at work on the website is the use of colors and typeface; they make it unmistakable to the user that he or she has stumbled across Frank Lloyd Wright in cyberspace. Graphically, the site is also very geometric; linear and rectangular forms serve as the main building blocks for each page, resulting in a layout that complements Wright's architectural style.

But aesthetics aren't the website's only strong suit. Want to read up on the history of the Willey House? Just click the History tab from the main menu and gain access to a timeline, a historical archive, and even recollections from previous owners of the house. Under the Restoration link, users will find a journal tracking the progress of the project. There, they can also view the various restoration plans in store for the house, in order of priority.

Still, the most unique feature on the site is the massing model—a three-dimensional blueprint engine that shows, in more than 30 stages, how the house was laid out and later constructed. This section of the site is extremely memory intensive, so low-bandwidth users may not be able to view it properly. But, as Sikora explains, it was a sacrifice they had to make: "We made a decision early on that we wanted the site to do things others have not. On a phone line, most of the site is viewable, but the highlights would [require] very long load times. Nevertheless, we decided to be forward looking rather than backward compatible."

Continuing the Tradition

Sikora says that they have received some praise, though more often it is for the restoration of the house than for the website itself. Nonetheless, he explains, "Guests frequently see the house through the lens of the site without being distracted by the site," which establishes that perfect union between form and function. Wright would have been proud of these Design Guys.

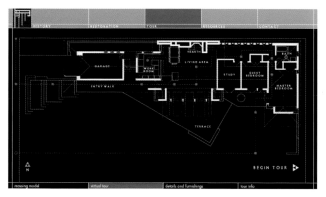

The Tour section includes a virtual tour, which takes users through the interior of the Willey House.

Aesthetics aren't the site's only strong suit, and this informative restoration journal is evidence of that.

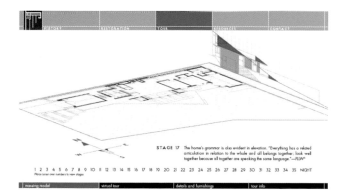

Arguably the most unique feature on the site, the massing model is an interactive blueprint that shows the various stages of Wright's creation.

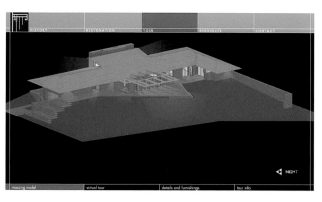

Some portions of the site are extremely memory intensive, but as Sikora explains, "We decided to be forward looking rather than backward compatible."

An optimistic future. Surrounding ourselves with people we love. A roof over our heads. A garden. Food. Clothing. Shelter. Having your basic needs met is important at any age, but perhaps even more so as we grow older. We all want to retain as much self-sufficiency as we can, yet we realize that as we get older, we simply need some help in some areas. How do we strike that balance? And how do we keep from worrying about a future that we know is growing shorter? How do we maintain our peace of mind that we've struggled so hard to achieve all our lives?

Camden provides housing for people. With more than 50,000 apartment homes in 145 communities across the United States, Camden has long been the leader in apartment home living. Many of these are apartment complexes are designed to fill the needs of those 60 years of age and up. However, Camden's image and name had not changed in more than two decades. As the multifamily residential real estate leader, the brand needed to evolve to stay on top.

Design Firm **Metal**
Client **Camden**
Project **Camden Brochure**

To create a lifestyle brand that would appeal to seniors, Metal created an optimistic, light, and airy feel that would bring peace of mind to the target audience. There is a certain comfort in still being able to ask "Why?" and "Why not?"

Working with a marketing team from Camden, Metal came up with a positioning for apartment living that creates a bright, inviting, and new lifestyle brand. Building a new corporate soul for the Camden brand involves everything from a new corporate paper system, a website, a massive intranet and extranet system design and development, a multitude of collateral/marketing materials, an interactive CD, the annual report, and an advertising campaign. The quantity of brochures produced is quite sizable, at times numbering up to 100,000 for a single print run. The brochures target residents as well as investors and employees. The design uniqueness and the materials used in the pieces is what makes the brochures so appealing.

Targeting seniors as a group means finding ways to make things that could be cliché not so cliché. As a lifestyle brand, it was important to show people within the Camden environment—for example, a woman is shown interacting with her grandson and his Gameboy. No fear of staying current for the older set here! Yet the surroundings are soft, warm, comforting, and the expression on the boy's face is a little poignant. The photo works so well because it could be a real moment. There is also a sense of peacefulness about the garden photo. It's lovely and quiet and rich, and the copy explains how Camden will perform all the maintenance, leaving you with peace of mind.

Peace of mind. Such a nice thing to have at any time, but especially as we grow older.

Rich, inviting—and very, very peaceful.

The attention to detail in this photo makes it seem very real and thus appealing. Everything feels comfortable — from the softness of the couch to the textured shirt, to the way that grandmother and grandson are interacting.

Involve the Reader

In this day and age, when "interactive" immediately calls to mind the latest new website with bells and whistles, is it possible for a regular, printed-on-paper brochure to be "interactive"?

IE Design proves that it is.

"Creative Solutions" is the name given to the design firm's corporate capabilities brochure, and it certainly is an apt name. Everything about it is a little unexpected, starting with the size. IE wanted the piece to be slightly oversized, but still able to fit in a file cabinet, so they chose to make it 9½" x 12" (24 cm x 30.5 cm). The brochure gets mailed to client contacts or anyone inquiring about IE Design. They also use it as a leave-behind at new client pitches or meetings.

Tell a Story

First and foremost, IE wanted the piece to captivate the reader, a task deemed even more important than conveying a bit of the design firm's personality and talents. The decision was made to have a "story" run horizontally through the book with interesting anecdotes and print techniques. It was a successful way to not only visually showcase their portfolio, but the format of the piece displayed IE's creativity.

With die cuts, short sheets, unusual printing techniques, and varied paper stock throughout, the piece feels truly "interactive" in the best possible sense of the word. Marcie Carson of IE Design explains, "The interactive quality speaks to our personality as well as our creativity. We like to have fun with what we do. I think the playful format conveyed this."

DESIGNS THAT STAND UP SPEAK OUT AND CANT BE IGNORED

What makes you tick? What makes you laugh? What makes you inspired? Although most design firms speak only about themselves, this brochure uses clever ideas like this small, three-page insert to talk to the reader directly about what they like.

In the End

There was a slight glitch in getting the logo on the cover to be dark enough, but that was nothing compared to the timing. Even when the design firm *is* the client—or possibly *because* the design firm is the client—there is often a problem meeting the deadline. The brochure ended up not being printed and sent out until a couple of months after they hoped it would.

When asked how long it took to produce, Marcie responds with the sigh of a true creative: "I was totally absorbed by this brochure. It was all I thought about night and day for weeks. It's a huge challenge to design for yourself. Without making it sound overly dramatic, it really becomes a process of self-awareness and soul searching. It felt like a year, but it was probably only about two months."

The piece ended up being quite costly, especially for such a small studio. But here too, "creative solutions" ended up being important. The printer gave them a great deal. And they also cooked up a little cost-saving juggling, as all the short sheets were printed at a small mom-and-pop printer and shipped to the larger printer for binding.

Although Marcie is ready to embark upon the process again by designing a new promotional piece, IE's director of business development is screaming, "No!" He says it's the best tool he has.

Even on the cover, the small arrow-like die cut speaks of the various design surprises to be found within.

The arrow theme continues as silver graphic design elements over a sepia tone photo. This spread highlights client testimonials.

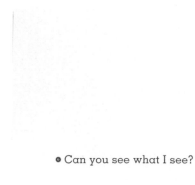

⊙ Can you see what I see?

A functional yet innovative way to always be able to keep the piece updated—the case studies are printed separately and put in a pocket so they can be adapted as needed without redoing the entire brochure.

Design Firm Blue River Design
Client MetroMail
Project We Love Mail Campaign

Everyone Loves a Good Game

Anyone who has ever played Spin the Bottle—a game popularized by kiss-hungry kids and drunken students—might think that it would be difficult to sell a promotion based on that game to a direct mail client.

Luckily, even direct mail marketers have a sense of humor.

Blue River Design, in Newcastle, England, had gotten a brief from their client, MetroMail. The brief was to attract the attention of targeted direct mail marketers and to introduce them to MetroMail in a lighthearted and unusual way so they would be receptive to a follow-up telephone call. They wanted to do something that would stand out in the mailing industry (which usually promotes themselves in a dry, straightforward way) and show that MetroMail was passionate about the work they do.

It was that idea of being passionate that sparked the idea behind the promotions. The first, the Engagement Ring mailer, consists of a red ring box, a toy engagement ring, and a small leaflet inside the box. It was mailed out in a small white box that was sealed with a MetroMail branded sticker. A booklet inside offered the receiver a "proposal" to form a meaningful relationship with MetroMail.

MetroMail's We Love Mail campaign has featured a range of different pieces since it was implemented by Blue River, including press advertising, exhibition stands, a calendar, interactive flash games, and multiple printed and three-dimensional mailers. These two provocative mailers demonstrate the company's passion for direct mail.

To keep the humor of the piece amid the sales benefits of MetroMail, the game featured a number of Office Dares. An example: "Say to your boss 'like your style' and pretend to shoot him with double-barreled fingers."

Game Time

The Spin the Bottle game mailer was sent to targeted direct mail marketers as an invitation to MetroMail's booth at a large direct marketing trade fair in the UK.

It was mailed out in a large, bright red tube that contained a branded bottle, a game board with playing instructions, and a reply mechanism. The aim of the MetroMail version of the game was to spin the bottle to find your perfect partner at the trade fair. The perfect partner, of course, was none other than MetroMail. The information on the game board outlined different benefits and services of choosing MetroMail and also featured office dares (such as "Ask the next eight people you work with 'Have you been working out?'") to make the mailer a bit provocative.

Blue River had no qualms about presenting such a provocative concept to the client. In fact, they were confident that both the Engagement Ring mailer and the Spin the Bottle mailer would be received well and were reluctant to submit a more toned-down version. MetroMail, the client, appreciated the humor and felt that it fit well with the overall campaign concept of "We Love Mail." They understood that the humor in this case is simply a vehicle to make MetroMail stand out from the crowd before the receiver is immediately presented with the attractive benefits of using MetroMail's services.

Addicted to Gaming

Blue River received immediate feedback from MetroMail that one of the UK's leading media companies called to say that office staff had been playing Spin the Bottle for an entire morning. It was the only direct mail invite that didn't end up in the bin. See what a little passion can do!

Although humor is often a hard sell (with some people simply not getting the joke), the mailers and the campaign as a whole have a great deal of serious sales messages and customer benefits.

Design Firm   **Blockdot**

Client   **Motorola**

Project   **Motorola Bobblehead Promotion**

Bobbleheads. It's hard to not laugh at bobbleheads.

So when Motorola wanted to include a game on a website that reinforced their position as the "Official Wireless Communications Sponsor of the NFL," Blockdot approached the game with a humorous twist and designed the NFL players as bobblehead dolls.

Rather than creating the same-old passing and kicking game, the bobblehead approach not only gave the game a refreshing new look, but there was a natural tie in—bobblehead dolls were given away as stadium promotional items.

Don't Drop the Ball

Motorola wanted to target technically savvy adults 18–50 years old, people who were both sports fans and mobile phone users. The original strategy was to create an online component to drive traffic to Motorola's site and collect user data. And the new buzzword in online advertising promotions is advergaming, a phrase that Blockdot knows well. In fact, Blockdot founders Dan Ferguson and Mike Bielinski are credited by many in the field as having created some of the first popular advergames of the nineties.

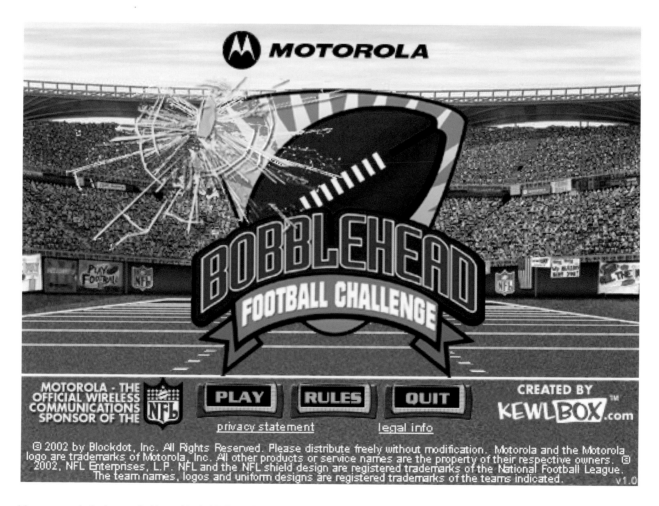

Advergame: an electronic game that is combined with the marketing savvy of an advertising campaign. In this case, the game showcases the Motorola and NFL branding as well as product placement of the wireless headsets throughout the game.

An advergame is exactly what it sounds like: an electronic game that is combined with the marketing savvy of an advertising campaign. Fun, engaging, and sought after by consumers, they are helpful at both driving traffic to a site and increasing brand awareness. In this case, the game showcases the Motorola and NFL branding as well as product placement of the wireless headsets throughout the game.

The bobblehead game was distributed via email from Motorola to the player. The game also included an email component that allowed players to send the game to their friends with a challenge to beat their score, creating a viral effect. That is, it was more apt to catch on with users beyond the original target. The game also felt individualized to the players, because each player can select his favorite team. The scores are then ranked based on each team. So not only are players posting scores individually, their teams are competing too.

A Technology Win

One thing that designers in the online arena learn quickly: if the technology doesn't fit the needs of the designer, it may be time to invent a technology that does. In this case, Blockdot knew it wanted to keep the file size down to a reasonable 3,000 KB so that it would be easy to email. So Blockdot created a technology that automatically created the graphics for the player's uniform to be the same as whatever NFL team the player selected. This color shifting allowed Blockdot to use a base image for the player instead of creating individual graphics for each team, keeping the file size to a minimum.

With 425,000 game plays to date and an average user experience of 16 minutes per game, it appears that the target audience was crazy for bobbleheads.

Bobbleheads. It's hard to not laugh at bobbleheads.

Rather than creating the same-old passing and kicking game, the bobblehead approach gave the game a refreshing new look.

The game reinforced Motorola's position as the "Official Wireless Communications Sponsor of the NFL."

Directory

Amoeba Corp.
457 Richmond St. West
Toronto, ON M5V 1X9 Canada
Tel: 416-599-2699
Fax: 416-599-2391
Email: kelar@amoebacorp.com
(Michael Kelar)
www.amoebacorp.com
16, 72

Angelini Design
Via del Colosseo 23
00184 Rome, Italy
Tel: +39 06-4620-641
Fax: +39 06-4360-6421
Email: roma@angelinidesign.com
www.angelinidesign.com
86

Anvil Graphic Design, Inc.
2611 Broadway St.
Redwood City, CA 94063 USA
Tel: 650-261-6094
Fax: 650-261-6095
Email: aratliff@hitanvil.com
(Alan Ratliff)
www.anvilpaper.com or www.hitanvil.com
80

Bisqit Design
5 Theobalds Rd.
London, WCIX 8SH UK
Tel: +44 020-7413-3739
Fax: +44 020-7413-3738
Email: daphne@bisqit.co.uk
(Daphne Diamant)
www.bisqit.co.uk
126

Blockdot
824 Exposition, Suite 2
Dallas, TX 75226 USA
Tel: 214-823-0500
Fax: 214-823-0535
Email: dferguson@blockdot.com
(Dan Ferguson)
www.blockdot.com
156

Blue River Design
The Foundry, Forth Banks
Newcastle Upon Tyne, NE1 3PA UK
Tel: +44 0191-261-0000
Fax: +44 0191-261-0010
Email: simon@blueriver.co.uk
(Simon Douglas)
www.blueriver.co.uk
94, 154

Bubblan Design (Studio Bubblan AB)
Sjunde Villagatan 28
50454 Boras, Sweden
Tel: +46 33-414441
Fax: +46 33-132968
Email: kari@bubblan.se (Kari Palmqvist)
www.bubblan.se
30

Cahan & Associates
171 2nd St., Suite 500
San Francisco, CA 94105 USA
Tel: 415-621-0915
Fax: 415-621-7642
Email: info@cahanassociates.com
www.cahanassociates.com
46

Carter Wong Tomlin
29 Brook Mews North
London, W2 3BW UK
Tel: +44 020 7569-0000
Fax: +44 020 7569-0001
Email: p.carter@carterwongtomlin.com
(Philip Carter)
www.carterwongtomlin.com
32

Chimera Design
6/179 Barkly St.
St. Kilda, Victoria 3182 Australia
Tel: +61 03-9593-6844
Fax: +61 03-9593-6855
Email: design@chimera.com.au
www.chimera.com.au
10

Design Guys
119 N 4th St., Suite 400
Minneapolis, MN 55401 USA
Tel: 612-338-4462
Fax: 612-338-1875
Email: steve@designguys.com
(Steve Sikora)
www.designguys.com
148

deepend
813 Broadway, 2nd Fl.
New York, NY 10003 USA
Tel: 212-253-1974
Fax: 212-253-2375
Email: iti@deepend.com (Iti Sakharet)
www.deepend.com
12, 134

Dinnick + Howells
298 Markham St., 2nd Fl.
Toronto, ON M6J 2G6 Canada
Tel: 416-921-5754
Fax: 416-921-0719
Email: Jonathan@dinnickandhowells.com
(Jonathan Howells)
www.dinnickandhowells.com
22, 112

Doppelganger, Inc.
180 Varick St., #1002
New York, NY 10014 USA
Tel: 212-807-1344
Fax: 212-807-7002
Email: Steininger@mindspring.com
(Otto Steininger)
www.ottosteininger.com
124

Dotzero Design
208 SW Stark St., #307
Portland, OR 97204 USA
Tel: 503-892-9262
Fax: 503-228-9403
Email: jonw@dotzerodesign.com
(Jon Wippich)
www.dotzerodesign.com
44, 138

Double You
Calle Esglesia 4-10, 3-A
08024 Barcelona, Spain
Tel: +34 93-292-31-10
Fax: +34 93-292-21-97
Email: barcelona@doubleyou.com
www.doubleyou.com
130, 132

Duffy Design (London)
67–69 Beak St.
London W1F 9SW UK
Tel: +44 0207-434-3919
Fax: +44 0207-434-3923
Email: info@duffy.com
www.duffy.com
56

Duffy Design (Minneapolis)
50 S. 6th St., Suite 2800
Minneapolis, MN 55402 USA
Tel: 612-758-2333
Fax: 612-758-2334
Email: info@duffy.com
www.duffy.com
64

Dynamo Art & Design
14 Plain St.
Natick, MA 01760 USA
Tel: 617-461-8811
Fax: 208-493-7895
Email: nw@dynamodesign.com
www.dynamodesign.com
106

Elfen
20 Harrowby Ln.
Cardiff Bay, CF10 5GN UK
Tel: +44 029-2048-4824
Fax: +44 029-2048-4823
Email: post@elfen.co.uk
www.elfen.co.uk
108

Emery Vincent Design
Level 1, 15 Foster St.
Surry Hills
Sydney NSW 2010 Austrailia
Tel: +61 2-9280-4233
Fax: +61 2-9280-4266
Email: sharon.nixon@evd.com.au
(Sharon Nixon)
www.evd.com.au
74, 88

Evolve
Studio 6, 42 Orchard Rd.
Highgate, London N6 5TR UK
Tel: +44 0208-340-9541
Fax: +44 0208-340-9634
Email: jh@evolvedesign.co.uk
(Jonathan Hawkes)
www.evolvedesign.co.uk
110

Frost Design London
The Gymnasium
56 Kings Way Pl.
Sans Walk, London EC1R 0LU UK
Tel: +44 020-7490-7994
Fax: +44 020-7490-7995
Email: info@frostdesign.co.uk
www.frostdesign.co.uk
28

Giorgio Davanzo Design
232 Belmont Ave. E, #506
Seattle, WA 98102 USA
Tel: 206-328-5031
Fax: 206-324-3592
Email: info@davanzodesign.com
www.davanzodesign.com
104

Hesse Design
Duesseldorfer Str. 16
40699 Erkrath, Germany
Tel: +49 211-280-7200
Fax: +49 211-2807-2020
Email: duesseldorf@hesse-design.de
www.hesse-design.de
102

Hornall Anderson Design Works
1008 Western Ave., Suite 600
Seattle, WA 98104 USA
Tel: 206-467-5800
Fax: 206-467-6411
Email: c_arbini@hadw.com
(Christina Arbini)
www.hadw.com
62, 96

Howalt Design Studio, Inc.
527 W. Scott Ave.
Gilbert, AZ 85233 USA
Tel: 480-558-0390
Fax: 480-558-0391
Email: howalt@qwest.net (Paul Howalt)
www.HowaltDesign.com
www.PaulHowalt.com
76

IE Design
422 Pacific Coast Highway
Hermosa Beach, CA 90254 USA
Tel: 310-376-9600
Fax: 310-727-3515
Email: mail@iedesign.net
www.iedesign.net
136, 152

Iridium, a design agency
43 Eccles St., 2nd Fl.
Ottawa, ON K1R 6S3 Canada
Tel: 613-748-3336
Fax: 613-748-3372
Email: mario@iridium192.com (Mario Lecuyer)
www.iridium192.com
118, 120

Iron Design
120 North Aurora St., Suite 5A
Ithaca, NY 14850 USA
Tel: 607-275-9544
Fax: 607-275-0370
Email: todd@irondesign.com (Todd Edmonds)
www.irondesign.com
122

Jack Morton Worldwide
498 Seventh Ave.
New York, NY 10018 USA
Tel: 212-401-7333
Fax: 212-401-7016
Email: anya_beaupre@jackmorton.com
www.jackmorton.com
144

Kinetic Singapore
2 Leng Kee Rd.
Thye Hong Centre, #04–03A
Singapore 159086 Singapore
Tel: +65 6379-5320
Fax: +65 6472-5440
Email: roy@kinetic.com.sg (Roy Poh)
www.kinetic.com.sg
116

Kolegram Design
37 Saint-Joseph Blvd., Gatineau
Hull, PQ J84 3V8, Canada
Tel: 819-777-5538
Fax: 819-777-8525
Email: mike@kolegram.com (Mike Teixeira)
www.kolegram.com
60, 146

Lewis Moberly
33 Gresse St.
London, W1T 1QU, UK
Tel: +44 020-7580-9252
Fax: +44 020-7255-1671
Email: nicola.shellswell@lewismoberly.com
www.lewismoberly.com
26

Metal
1210 W. Clay, Suite 18
Houston, TX 77019 USA
Tel: 713-523-5177
Fax: 713-523-5176
Email: info@metal.cc
www.metal.cc
36, 150

Nesnadny + Schwartz
10803 Magnolia Dr.
Cleveland, OH 44106 USA
Tel: 216-791-7721
Fax: 216-791-3654
Email: info@nsideas.com
www.nsideas.com
42, 142

Nolin Branding and Design
1610, Sainte-Catherine St. West, Bureau 500
Montreal, PQ H3H 2S2 Canada
Tel: 514-846-2541
Fax: 514-939-7343 or
2 Bloor St. W., 29th Fl.
Toronto, ON M4W 3R6 Canada
Tel: 416-413-8901
Fax: 416-972-5656
Email: info@nolin.ca
www.nolin.ca
58

Noon
592 Utah St.
San Francisco, CA 94110 USA
Tel: 415-621-4922
Fax: 415-621-4966
Email: info@designatnoon.com
www.designatnoon.com
82

Origin
Chetham House
Bird Hall Ln.
Cheadle Heath, Cheshire SK3 0ZP UK
Tel: +44 0161-495-4808
Fax: +44 0161-495-4567
Email: Adam@origincreativedesign.com (Adam Lee)
www.origincreativedesign.com
128

Ph.D
1524A Cloverfield Blvd.
Santa Monica, CA 90404 USA
Tel: 310-829-0900
Fax: 310-829-1859
Email: phd@phdla.com
www.phdla.com
98, 100

Plazm Media
P. O. Box 2863
Portland, OR 97208 USA
Tel: 503-528-8000
Fax: 503-528-8092
Email: josh@plazm.com (Joshua Berger)
www.plazm.com
50, 68

R2 Design
Praceta D Nuno Alvares Pereira
20 2 Box
4450 218 Matosinhos, Portugal
Tel: +351 229-386-865
Fax: +351 229-350-838
Email: info@rdois.com
www.rdois.com
14, 34

Red Canoe
347 Clear Creek Trail
Deer Lodge, TN 37726 USA
Tel: 423-965-2223
Fax: 423-965-1005
Email: studio@redcanoe.com
www.redcanoe.com
84

Renegade Marketing Group
75 Ninth Ave, 4th Fl.
New York, NY 10016 USA
Tel: 646-486-7700
Fax: 646-486-7800
Email: dneisser@renegademarketing.com (Drew Neisser)
www.renegademarketing.com
48

Riordon Design
131 George St.
Oakville, ON L6J 3B9 Canada
Tel: 905-339-0750
Fax: 905-339-0753
Email: ric@riordondesign.com (Ric Riordon)
www.riordondesign.com
78

Sandstrom Design
808 SW Third Ave., Suite 610
Portland, OR 97204 USA
Tel: 503-248-9466
Fax: 503-227-5035
Email: rick@sandstromdesign.com
www.sandstromdesign.com
70, 90

Squires & Company
2913 Canton St.
Dallas, TX 75226 USA
Tel: 214-939-9194
Fax: 214-939-3464
Email: murphy@squirescompany.com
www.squirescompany.com
54

stilradar
Schwabstr. 10A
70197 Stuttgart, Germany
Tel: +49 0711-887-5520
Fax: +49 0711-882-2344
Email: info@stilradar.de
www.stilradar.de
114

Strawberry Frog
Tesselschadestraat 13
1054 ET Amsterdam, The Netherlands
Tel: +31 20-5300-400
Fax: +31 20-5300-499
Email: mark@blueberryfrog.com (Mark Chalmers)
www.blueberryfrog.com
8, 38

SullivanPerkins
2811 McKinney Ave., Suite 320
Dallas, TX 75204 USA
Tel: 214-922-9080
Fax: 214-922-0044
Email: rob.wilson@sullivanperkins.com (Rob Wilson)
www.sullivanperkins.com
20

Templin Brink Design
720 Tehama St.
San Francisco, CA 94103 USA
Tel: 415-255-9295
Fax: 415-255-9296
Email: info@templinbrinkdesign.com
www.templinbrinkdesign.com
66

Terrapin Graphics
991 Avenue Rd.
Toronto, ON M5P 2K9 Canada
Tel: 416-932-8832
Fax: 416-487-2122
Email: james@terrapin-graphics.com (James Peters)
www.terrapin-graphics.com
18

Viva Dolan Communications & Design Inc.
99 Crown's Ln., Suite 500
Toronto, ON M5R 3P4 Canada
Tel: 416-923-6355
Fax: 416-923-8136
Email: frank@vivadolan.com (Frank Viva)
www.vivadolan.com
92

Wasserman & Partners Advertising Inc.
Suite 160, 1020 Mainland St.
Vancouver, BC V6B 2T4 Canada
Tel: 604-684-1111
Fax: 604-408-7049
Email: knishi@wasserman-partners.com
www.wasserman-partners.com
52, 140

Wink
126 North 3rd St. #100
Minneapolis, MN 55401 USA
Tel: 612-630-5138
Fax: 612-455-2645
Email: richard@wink-mpls.com (Richard Boynton)
www.wink-mpls.com
40

Zoesis, Inc.
246 Walnut St., Suite 301
Newton, MA 02460 USA
Tel: 617-969-5700
Fax: 617-969-4472
Email: joe@zoesis.com or laura@zoesis.com
www.zoesis.com
24

About the Author

Lisa Hickey is founder and CEO of Velocity Inc., a Boston, Massachusetts, advertising and brand engineering firm. She has been creating innovative, memorable, and brand-defining advertising for the past fifteen years. Her work has been recognized with the industry's highest honors, including awards from Clio, Cannes, Hatch, NEBA, the London Show, *Communication Arts*, and has been included in Marquis' *Who's Who* in the world. She teaches at Massachusetts College of Art and Emerson College, and is also a published poet.

Acknowledgments

Sometimes it takes a village to write a book. Many thanks to Brian Chin, whose long hours, attention to detail, and great thinking helped to make this book possible. Thanks to Penny Lam, Bruce Gray, Caitlin Hickey, Lynn McNamee, and Jennifer Falk, all of whom helped to create this book. And finally, thanks to everyone at the design firms around the world who created such remarkable promotions as well as those who expedited the process of pulling the materials together.

Ultimately, this book is dedicated to my family, Mark, Caitlin, John, Allie, and Shannon, who always give me the perfect amount of support, even when none is asked for.

DESIGNS THAT STAND UP SPEAK OUT AND CANT BE IGNORED